Wonders of the Himalayas

Wonders of the Himalayas

SIR FRANCIS YOUNGHUSBAND

GYAN

Published by

GYAN

Gyan Publishing House
5, Ansari Road
Daryaganj, New Delhi-110002
Phone: 011-47034999, 9811692060
E-mail: books@gyanbooks.com

Distribution Network
gyanbooks.com
India, USA, Canada, UK, Australia, France

ISBN : 978-81-212-4227-1 (PB)
First Published, 1862

2nd Impression 2020

Printed at: Gyan Press, Delhi.

The book at your disposal is the edition of an old book originally published long back. The Text quality of this book may not be at par as compared to our other books but many readers approached us to reprint this important book so that it could satiate their hunger. We request all the readers of this book to help us to improve its quality by providing the necessary text of those pages which are not properly visible. Your valuable support in this case will be highly appreciated and acknowledged and our future readers will be benefitted immensely.

PREFACE

WHEN I recently wrote a book on what is to me by far the most important and interesting thing in life—namely, religion—I was peremptorily ordered by more than one reviewer to leave religion to the divines. If I had written a book on politics, I would not have been told to leave politics to professional politicians. But religion! Religion is no concern of a traveller. It must be left to professionals. So because I have travelled I must not write about religion. It is a sad penalty for the sin of travelling. But reviewers have to be obeyed. And it so happened that at the very time when they were issuing their edicts to me a friend chanced to remark that he would like to look inside my head and see some of my experiences, and he asked me why I did not write a book for boys. It was an enticing suggestion. But I doubt if boys read books written for boys. They like books written for men. So this is a book written for men, but which, I hope, boys may read, for it is about adventures I had when I was not much more than a boy myself.

F. E. Y.

December, 1923.

CONTENTS

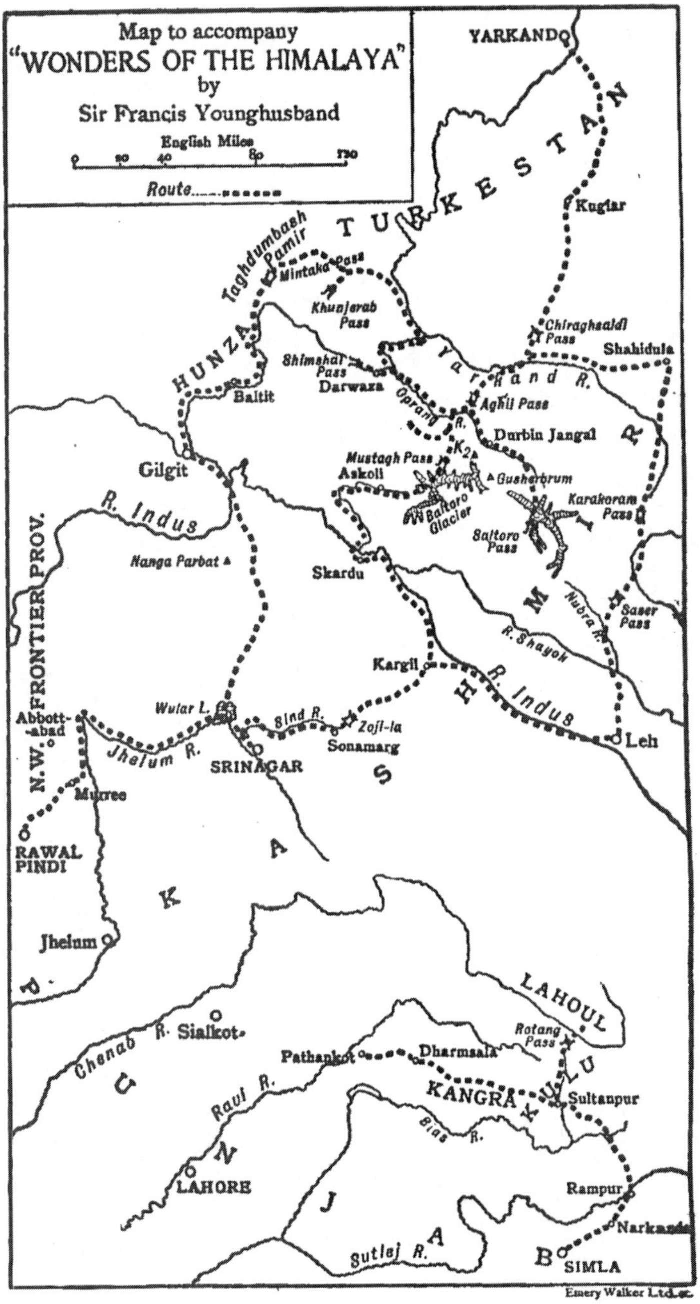

Emery Walker Ltd. sc.

WONDERS OF THE HIMALAYA

CHAPTER I

FIRST LEAVE IN THE HIMALAYA

IN the distance we see a range of hazy hills. We do not doubt their real existence. But they are shrouded in a bluey mystery. And we long to penetrate their secret. Glorious woods, with marvellous birds and beautiful flowers, they must surely contain. And magnificent views we should see over wonderful country ahead. We cannot be content until we have stood upon those hills and seen the other side.

Of all mountain ranges the most wonderful is the Himalaya, besides being the highest; and it provides wonders in the greatest variety—variety of outward form; of flower and forest; of beast and bird and insect; and of human races. So impressive, indeed, is it that the Indians have always looked upon it with awe and reverence. And we who have known it best are most impressed. By rare good fortune I have been able to live in the Himalayan Mountains for years together, to explore them up and down from one side to another, backwards and forwards, year after year. And though I have already in books and lectures told the story of these wanderings, I do not seem yet to have told all that they have been to me—or told the most important part. However much I say, there always seems a great deal more to tell.

In the year 1884 I was quartered with my regiment, the King's Dragoon Guards, at Rawal Pindi, when one day in April, just as the hot weather was coming on, the adjutant informed me that, if I cared to take it, I might have two and a half months' leave; and he strongly recommended me to take it. This was joy indeed. I was not yet twenty-one. I had been two years in the regiment, and with drills and examinations had been kept pretty hard at work. Now came the chance for a real holiday. What should I do with it? There was not much doubt. Those who live in the plains in India naturally look to the hills. To the hills, therefore, I would go. The Himalayan Mountains were close at hand, so I determined to plunge right into them. Not, indeed, into that part which we could see from Rawal Pindi itself—an entrancing line of purple mountains crowned by spotless snowy peaks—but a part farther east and south near Dharmsala, where my uncle Robert Shaw had lived, and from whence he had planned those journeys which had carried him across the Himalaya to the plains of Turkestan beyond. He had died only half a dozen years before, and I knew I should find there men who had known him, and a few, perhaps, who had accompanied him on his journeys. And for me there hung about such men a wondrous halo of romance. My uncle had always been to me a hero, and had won his way deep into my heart by giving me half a sovereign when I was a boy at Clifton College. And if I could see even only his servants I should be able to picture to myself something of the hard adventure. And, better still, I should be able to gather something of the attachment my uncle felt for men who loyally served him. For besides being a quite exceptional linguist, proficient in most European languages, and versed in many Oriental tongues as well, Robert Shaw had a genius for attaching Asiatics to him. He always spoke and wrote in terms of warm affection of his men. And I was eager to see these men themselves, and perhaps hear from them something of their adventures and something, too, of their devotion to my uncle.

So, as I say, it was to Dharmsala, roughly midway between Kashmir and Simla, that I determined to go when I had this holiday almost thrust upon me. And what more heavenly chance could a young man have? The weather in April and May would be perfect. There would be unbroken sunshine day after day. Yet I need suffer no excessive heat, for I could just climb higher as the heat increased. Then I would get right up under the glorious peaks. I would see glaciers and stupendous precipices and rushing rivers and dashing waterfalls, and great cedar forests and flowers I had never seen before, and strange hillmen. John Alexander, a brother officer who had been there, said I would have a splendid time, and became as keen on my small adventure as I was myself, offering me both money and a rifle.

And I might have gone on a shooting expedition; but the sportsman's instinct is missing in me. I have an enormous admiration for those many men one sees in India who will for weeks and weeks, every year, give up all comforts, spend all their spare cash, undergo the severest hardships, and run the most deadly risks in the pursuit of game. I know well the strong determination, the hard training, the fine physique, the skill, and the steadiness of nerve that is required by the sportsman who will himself seek out the tiger in the plains of India, or the Kashmir stag, the ibex, markhor, or *Ovis ammon* in the Himalaya. Only real men can do this. And manliness we all admire. And the joy they get from a successful stalk—from successfully pitting their wits against the wits of the animal—we must all envy.

Yet I do not regret the absence in me of the sportsman's instinct. What I do most heartily regret is that my instinct for natural history was never fostered during youth and childhood. There must be very few in whom the love of living things is wholly absent. Certainly I can recall it in me from my earliest days. I can feel to this day the joy I felt, when five or six years old, at finding white violets in a Somersetshire wood and a little red cup in the moss of a Somersetshire lane; at watching sea anemones in the pools of the Ilfracombe rocks; at seeing rabbits on a summer evening scurrying in and out of their holes on the grassy edge of a Devonshire wood; at discovering a cosy tomtit's nest one Easter holiday; at trapping and holding in my hands a delightful little chaffinch; and, above all, at collecting butterflies one summer holiday in Switzerland. From all these incidents I derived intense enjoyment. I did not want to kill the chaffinch. But I did most keenly want to hold it in my hands and admire it more nearly than was possible when it was still at liberty. And the butterflies I wanted for the sake of the sheer joy there was in having between my finger and thumb something so beautiful, so rare, and so difficult to find and catch. So, like most boys, I had the nascent naturalist spirit in me. But also like most boys I was wrenched violently away from opportunities of developing it and of observing and getting to love the animals and birds and flowers about us, and was with other boys herded into class-rooms and forced to strain my brains in acquiring quantities of quite useless information.

But if I had none of the sportsman's instinct and if the naturalist instinct had been nearly atrophied within me, I had—Heaven be praised—the explorer's instinct still strong and ardent. That was more than the most fervent examiner could deaden. It was born in me, and it had been fostered by circumstance. It was born in me because both on my father's and my mother's side my progenitors had been accustomed to travel over the earth. And it was fostered in me, for while my parents were in India I was taken away during the holidays for tours in North Wales, Cornwall, Devonshire, and Somersetshire. And when they returned we spent many holidays in Switzerland and the south of France.

Hence the zest with which I started on my first leave in India. A night's journey by train brought me to Amritsar, and a few hours on a branch line brought me to Pathankote at the foot of the hills from whence my journey on foot of about forty miles to Dharmsala would commence. And this was the true beginning of my life of exploration. Here I was at last absolutely free—for two months, anyhow. And here I was at last entirely by myself—in real solitude. And young men do need a breathing space now and then in which to be alone, to be by themselves, in order to find themselves and be themselves. As boys they are hurried off to school, herded up with a crowd of other boys, and constrained into a mould whether they fit it or not, and regardless of whether the mould is bruising some of their most sensitive parts. Before they know anything of the world they are again rushed off—this time into a profession or business—and again a mould is applied. They do need, therefore, a time now and then to themselves—a time quite free of the pressure of their fellows in which they can indulge their own individuality, find their own feet, and expand upon the lines they are naturally disposed to develop.

Something of this feeling I had as I set out the next morning on my march to Dharmsala. And I felt, too, like a man feels when the motor-car at last stops and he can get out and stretch his legs, and look at the view, and look into the hedgerows and really see life, instead of being at the mercy of a machine and a mechanic, rushed through life without a chance of enjoying the beauties on the way.

I suppose I must have suffered the usual irritation of the dak-bungalow khansama who would produce the toughest old cock and call it chicken, and who would have my breakfast at seven when I was wanting it at six, so as to enjoy the freshness of the dawn; or of the mulemen bringing their mules late, or loitering on the march. It is certain that I must have had many such irritations, and no doubt expressed my feelings at the moment. But these are not the things that linger long in one's memory. The impressions which have lasted are very different. First the beauty of those early mornings. I was in the "foot-hills" of the Himalaya, among the buttresses, as it were, of the mighty range which lay behind, but which was not yet visible. I was perhaps a thousand feet or so above the plains of India. And now, in the middle of April, the air at sunrise was cool and fresh. There was no nip or bite in it, but it was pure and invigorating, and so clear that I could see far away along the foot-hills, and far away over the plains. And there was never a cloud. But over all was the lovely delicate haze of varying lilac and purple which gives the charm and mystery to every mountain region. As I stepped out on my first day's march in the Himalaya, a strange exhilaration thrilled me. I kept squeezing my fist together and saying emphatically to myself and to the universe at large: "Oh, *yes!* Oh, *yes!* This really *is*. How splendid! How splendid!" Life to me did indeed seem worth living. The world really was beautiful—something I could really love.

And it was not a case of "every prospect pleasing," and only man being vile. For man was not vile. Man was very attractive. These foot-hills in the northern part of the Himalaya are inhabited by manly races, who have maintained both their independence and the purity of their stock while waves of invasion have been surging over the plains below them. Here we meet some of the most ancient families of Rajputs, the nobility of India, highborn-looking men, rulers and soldiers, dignified in their bearing and with conscious pride of lineage. And among the Mohamedans are many of a truly patriarchal type, with grace and ease of manner, who would have stood for any Biblical character. And though I did not know it, there had arisen in this district, just about the time I was passing through it, a man who was honestly convinced he was both the Messiah of the Christians and the Mahdi of the Mohamedans, and was destined therefore by God to combine both Mohamedans and Christians under his leadership. Many thousands of people believed in him. But he had a strong prejudice against native Christians. He used to prophesy the death of certain native Christians within a year, and as the deaths actually occurred the English missionary prosecuted him in a court of law. During his trial he made a dramatic appeal to the English judge, declaring himself to be like Christ before Pilate, and he was acquitted; and in consequence of his acquittal he always afterwards spoke in terms of the warmest praise of British justice. But, years after, the judge told me that there was a pretty strong suspicion that the prophet's followers had in some manner or other made away with the native Christians named, but that no legal proof could be established. So he had the prophet up privately and warned him against prophesying in future—or if he must prophesy then he must take care that his prophecies did not come true. The prophet took the warning and the death-rate among native Christians decreased.

Gradually ascending through these foot-hills, and passing every now and then some fort picturesquely perched on an outstanding rock, or some ancient temple designed on the model of bamboos bending over towards one another across a roadway, I reached Dharmsala on the third day, and went straight to Robert Shaw's house on the top of a little hill a mile or so outside. Now, indeed, I was in a thick atmosphere of exploration. The house itself was named Easthome, and was one which Shaw had occupied when managing the tea plantations which lay all around it. Being prevented by an attack of rheumatic fever—the disease from which he eventually died as Resident at Mandalay when only thirty-nine—from joining the Army, he had joined my father and mother in India and set up as a tea planter. And it was from here that he had planned his great journey to Yarkand in 1869, designing to sell his tea in Turkestan and to bring back from there carpets, felts and silks. Commercially the journey was not of much success, but scientifically and politically it had much value. He was awarded the Gold Medal of the Royal Geographical Society, and he was taken into the political service of the Government of India.

As it was only a dozen years since his last visit to Yarkand, there were still many who had known him, and some who had accompanied him; and these soon collected round me. Towards these men I had a feeling very akin to awe. It was to me something wonderful that these very men had traversed the succession of ranges which separated India from Turkestan, and had clambered up the glaciers, plunged through icy streams, crossed passes 18,000 and 19,000 feet above sea-level, risked the dangers of life among hostile peoples, and seen the mysterious cities of distant Central Asia. I looked upon them with the greatest reverence—staid, grave, dignified figures, with faces worn by strain and hardship; and with a characteristic composure and politeness. I was quite happy in simply looking on them. But I liked also to hear them speak of Shaw. And their faces kindled into eager life when they spoke of "Shah-sahib." He was their "father and their mother." He was always kind to them and looked after them, and had provided them with pensions. The attachment and devotion of these hillmen to Englishmen whom they can trust and who will be thoughtful of them is one of the most touching traits in human nature. And if I had first felt awe for them on account of their adventures, I now felt real reverence for them on account of their fidelity, loyalty and affection.

But in my uncle's house I found not only men but books. And books can also inspire a traveller. First there was my uncle's own book, "High Tartary and Yarkand," published by John Murray in 1871. In those days books of travel were illustrated by real pictures and not by mere photographs. And pictures play an important part in impressing the imagination. The frontispiece of

Shaw's book is a picture in colour of a peak in the Kuen-lun range, and it set me craving to see such a peak towering up to one sharp pinnacle point across a chasm of terrific precipices. Then there was another picture of an inundation caused by the melting of a glacier, with men hanging on by the skin of their teeth to a boulder, while a great river was surging all round them, carrying along with it huge blocks of ice from the glacier which formed the background. How splendid, I thought it would be, to have such an adventure! And, as a fact, three years later I did have exactly such an experience.

Shaw's book naturally first appealed. But there were two others which profoundly affected me. I cannot now remember their names, but the one was by Humboldt and the other was by General Sabine. And the point about them was that I got from them for the first time in my life an impression of the world as a whole. All our education used to be snippety and fragmentary. I never got to look at the world in what may be called its togetherness. We were not taught about even mankind as a whole. We used to learn about a century or two of Greek history, a century or two of Roman history, a century or two of English history—nothing about Indian history—nothing about the human race in its entirety. Then a little geography, a very little geology, a few facts about astronomy, a smattering of physics and chemistry; and, on Sunday, a great deal about the Israelites. But about the world as a whole—nothing. About the relation of the individual man to the world as a whole—nothing. Yet this is the essential thing a man should know. The one thing about which he should have the fullest knowledge is our relationship to the world in which we find ourselves. These books of Humboldt and Sabine did not deal exhaustively with this fundamental problem, but they did deal with the connection of the earth with the stars, and the connection of the features of the earth with the plants and animals, and of the plants and animals with man. And I got the first glimmering of a feeling for the world as a whole, of being wrapt up in the world, of being part and parcel of it, and of being swept along in its onward rush, and yet of having my own part to play in it too. And I felt instigated to go on finding out more about it.

I got together all the maps and route-books of the Himalaya I could find in my uncle's house, and had up men who knew the country round, and planned out my first little expedition into the Himalaya. I could, of course, in the two months at my disposal cover no new ground on the present occasion. Original exploration I could only plan for some grand future. Still, there was infinite delight in spreading out maps on a big table, stretching myself across them, tracing out a route to follow which would enable me to see the utmost in the time available, noting all the peaks marked 17,000, 18,000, and a few 20,000 feet, making pictures of them in my mind, and wondering whether any of them were like that picture of "A Peak in the Kuen-lun" in Robert Shaw's book; and then reading up all I could discover about the districts I should pass through, and filling up with my imagination what the exasperating writers had omitted to describe. The tantalising thing was that the highest peaks and the most stupendous gorges lay just beyond my reach. However, there was a sufficiency to see for the present, and I must possess my soul in patience till I could find, or more probably make, an opportunity for some real exploration and be able to see the true monarchs of the Himalaya.

√Leaving Dharmsala on April 30, I intended to make my way across the open Kangra Valley to the Swiss-like Kulu Valley, and on to the cold barren Valley of Lahoul, and thence back into Kulu and across the deep-cut valley of the Sutlej, and along the heights to Simla. There was, as I say, nothing new in this. But it was not a tourist-ridden route. Only now and then would I meet a European, and going on foot and being by myself I could absorb unto me—or perhaps it might be better expressed, create out of me—the true spirit of the Himalaya.

The Kangra Valley, through which I first passed, was bounded on my left-hand side—that is, the north-west—by the line of the Himalaya Mountains, and on my right by the last outer ridges separating the mountains from the perfectly level plains of India. The valley itself was roughly about 3,000 feet above sea-level. The line of mountains was fine, but it did not rise more than 16,000 feet above sea-level, and there were no single peaks of outstanding grandeur. On the whole it gave the impression of a wall guarding vast wonders behind it. I was filled not so much with admiration of what I saw as with curiosity to see what there was behind that wall. My spirit was eagerly pressing on to things not yet revealed.

Yet the valley itself had beauties of its own. Under the high noontide sun the little hills into which it was broken looked bare and brown and monotonous. But in the early morning and late evening they presented a very different picture. Then they glowed in varying colour and varying light and shade. Delicate blues and purples, lilacs and violets, greens and yellows suffused them, and long shadows showed up their varying relief.

A couple of mules carried my baggage. But I would leave them in charge of my servant and trudge on ahead independently, with two or three "chupatties"—flat pancake-like rounds of unleavened bread—in one pocket and a book in another. The country was richly cultivated, with thriving villages and an air of prosperity. Often by the roadside were almost English hedges of wild roses, both white and pink, now in full bloom. And on May 1 I stopped at Palampur, one of the prettiest places I know—almost like a park—with a bazaar at one end, and the houses of the European tea planters dotted about among the deodar cedars, firs and pines; while above the tops of the trees rose the pure white outline of the Himalayan rampart. The roads were wide and clean, and fenced in by bamboo trellises wreathed with roses. And a conspicuous object, surrounded with pines of varying colours and by a well-tended English garden, was a simple English church, a silent witness that Englishmen, however far removed from home, and however deeply engaged in earning a living for themselves and their families, still aspire after what will satisfy their souls.

This church, of course, was of quite recent construction; it cannot have been twenty years old. But on the following day, at Baijnath, I saw another witness to men's craving for satisfaction of their soul needs—a beautiful Hindu temple, centuries and centuries old, far older than Westminster Abbey. Yet, old though it was, it was still inviting to men—inviting even to me. The sun was shining warmly on it. Brightly clothed men were going in and out. Many more were seated in the precincts, talking together and enjoying themselves. A few sitting cross-legged on the ground, with the head and body bent, were deep in contemplation. It was not all sanctity and piety that one saw there. There was much grossness too. However that may be, men would not have built that temple, both so beautiful and so enduring, and men would not have wended their way thither, century after century, from the far plains of India if they had not found their satisfaction for some deep essential need.

From the most ancient times to the present day, the most primitive people, as well as the most advanced, have felt that behind what they see with their eyes, and can hold in their hands, and weigh and measure in the balance, there are hidden invisible powers at work in the world. Spiritual agencies of some kind are somehow and somewhere operating in the world and bringing about the happenings we experience. The thunder rolls, the lightning flashes, the rain descends in torrents and floods arise. Some invisible spirit must be at work to cause all this, they say. Sudden diseases come; men die in agony without any apparent reason: again, some unseen spiritual agency must be at work. But, on the other hand, the sun rises with unfailing regularity, the seasons follow one another in ordered succession, so there must also be some steadying power at work. And, most wonderful and inscrutable of all, when the seed is sown in the ground it ripens into wheat; when man and woman love, children are born of their love. Men cannot do these things of themselves. The most skilled mechanic and the most cunning artist combined could not create even a flower, much less a lamb, a calf, or a child. Invisibly at work in the world must be spiritual powers—perhaps all working under the control and direction of one Supreme Power—sometimes working for the good of men, sometimes, it would seem, for their harm. And what men through the ages have sought to know is how these powers—or this one Supreme Power—may be approached, to be propitiated, or to be got to help and not to hinder men.

And when men living in the plains of India saw the Himalaya rising to incredible heights, clothed in dim mysterious haze but culminating in summits of purest shining white, they came irresistibly to the conclusion that here indeed must be the abode of the powers which rule the world. Here, high above this soiled and groaning earth, must dwell those spiritual beings who affected men's destiny so mightily for good or ill. So the most intrepid among them proceeded to explore the Himalayan heights and to penetrate their inner depths. Ordinarily they would ascend a river to its source. A river brought to them both good and ill. In moderation its waters would fertilise their lands; in excess they would flood the land and bring destruction to man and beast, and all the works of man; in default their crops would wither under the burning sun of India. At the source of the river must surely then be found the spiritual power which could work such good or ill. But even at the source—perhaps at the mouth of some icy glacier—the adventurers would not come across this being face to face. They had ventured far, but of what they were in search they had seen with their bodily eyes no more than they had seen when in the plains of India. But those who had ventured so far were necessarily men of thought and imagination and determination, and what they had not been able to discover with their bodily eye they sought to discover with the eye of the soul. By using every faculty of the soul they meant to explore the spiritual mysteries of the world, and find out what the powers were like which directed and controlled her, and wherein did they dwell. And to this day men from the plains of India come in hundreds to the Himalaya on the self-same quest—on the quest especially of that one Supreme Spirit whom men all over the earth have come to think must control all minor spirits and rule the world—and rule her for the good: though many now would hold that the Spirit controls the world from within her and not from outside.

Not on this occasion, but on many others, I have

talked with these men. Some of them are genial souls. One I remember who, when I asked him whether he enjoyed the Himalaya, said: No, he didn't. There was nothing but wood and stones. No sugar-cane was grown. So few people gave him any sugar. But he had a little, he said, and he forthwith gave me some. Others are much more stern and austere, and really are absorbed in spiritual contemplation. And among these are men who have, with a fearful wrench, torn themselves from all comforts and pleasures of home and gone off without money, without possessions of any kind, without even clothing beyond the barest covering, to wander in the jungles of India, by the banks of its sacred rivers, stopping sometimes in caves, sometimes at shrines, sometimes in temples, mortifying the body, subduing the passions, meditating on God, striving to realise Him, seeking out great living masters, searching the sacred books, training and disciplining themselves till they in their turn come to be regarded as holy and to attract disciples to them. Many of the holy men who wander over India and make their way to the Himalaya are gross and coarse. And many domineer with insufferable spiritual arrogance. But a few there are of a sanctity most exquisite—men who in their ardent search for God have endured the most terrible hardships of body, mind and soul, and through their sufferings have acquired a gentleness and a sensitiveness of soul which wins men to them with irresistible attraction. And to them the proudest chiefs in India will tender their respectful homage, placing them in the seat of honour, and taking the lower place themselves. Such a one was Rama Krishna, whom I have described in "The Gleam," and who is revered to this day by the most enlightened men in India.

Of all this, as a young subaltern, I was unaware. None the less I could not help being impressed by that temple at Baijnath, so ancient, so grand and simple in its general outline, so rich and fine in its detailed carvings, so revered by the thousands of devoted pilgrims who have centred on it from every part of India in every single one of its thousand years and more of history.

CHAPTER II

BY KULU TO SIMLA

BESIDES pilgrims and holy men I would meet numbers of traders. There was no cart-road, so the goods—mostly grain, hides, piece-goods, and salt—were carried on pack animals, generally bullocks and camels. And in all my wanderings I have had a special feeling for those hardy traders who carry merchandise on pack animals across the mountains and accompany their goods themselves. Railway trains and motor-lorries are excellent things, and we could not do without them now. But the trader who sits in his office and trades by means of these is far removed from Nature. He has his comfort and convenience, but he has none of the thrill and excitement of the men who follow their animals over mountain and valley, in sunshine and in storm. Most of these traders I have found to be robust and cheery, excellent company, with plenty of intelligence and knowledge of men.

And in talking with these traders on the marches through Kangra there was continued in me that process of thawing towards the "natives" which my uncle's servants had first set going. For when I set out on my travels my opinion of natives in general was not high. I was fresh from a year's military training at Sandhurst and nearly two years with my regiment. And during those years strict punctuality, rigid order, and instantaneous execution of commands had been incessantly drilled into me. Moreover, as an officer, while I was reproved by my seniors—and reproved with a directness and force of language characteristic of those days—I had on my part to reprove others who were dilatory, slack, and below the standard of required smartness. Naturally, therefore, I was disposed to apply these standards to those outside my regiment. And it is little wonder that when I ordered my muleman to be ready to start at 6 a.m., and neither at 6 a.m. nor 6.15 nor 6.30 was he ready, I was disposed to use to him the language which would have been used to me in like circumstances. Whether I actually used such language or not I have no recollection. But from remarks entered in my diary I gather I had no high opinion of muleteers in general, and I rather think I said and did things of which I would now be heartily ashamed.

However, the native of India, if he has a quite enormous capacity for arousing the ire of the vigorous, competent Englishman, has also a singular capacity for winning his affection. He shows trust and faith in the Englishman, and the Englishman likes to be trusted. Better still, the Indian shows gratitude, and we are all grateful for gratitude. One evening, after I had made a double march—that is, walked about twenty-four miles—and had just turned comfortably into bed, my servant woke me up to say there was a man dying in the caravanserai near by, and his friends had begged that the Englishman would give him some medicine. So, knowing that the matter must be urgent or my servant would not have disturbed himself or me, I turned out of bed, walked over to the serai, and found a poor man lying on the ground evidently in great pain. I had not the slightest idea what was the matter with him; but I thought some chlorodyne would do him no harm, so I administered a dose and left some more to be given later on. Up till then the men about him had been wringing their hands and saying he was dying: and so he probably would have out of sheer despair. But as soon as I gave the medicine and asserted with the assurance of a youth of twenty that he would soon get all right, they shouted, "The Sahib has saved your life; to-morrow you will be well." And when I went the next morning he really was a different man. He said I had saved his life, and all the men began kissing my feet.

This is a common enough experience in travelling in the Himalaya: and when the people show such implicit faith in one, and show their gratitude in such a touching way, one's heart cannot help warming towards them. I regret that mine never warmed to anything like the degree of temperature it should have, I was always so dead intent upon my explorations. I seemed to lack enough repose of soul to warm to concrete individuals, however much I might to the individual in the abstract. But what warmth was lacking in me I have observed kindling brightly enough in others; and in the old Indian Army, as it was before the war, I have known officers who had a devotion to Indians which was not one whit less than their devotion to their own countrymen: General Bruce to the Gurkhas and Major Wallace Dunlop to the Sikhs are two I could name. General Bruce is well known now for his leadership of the Mount Everest Expedition, for which he was chosen largely on account of this very devotion to Gurkhas and knowledge of them. Major Wallace Dunlop never attained to high military fame. But he deserves being known for his absolute devotion to the Sikhs, and for his capacity for inspiring devotion in them to himself. If ever any man loved other men he loved his Sikhs; thought of their welfare; uprose in wrathful indignation if a thing was said or done against them; and cherished dearly in his heart every little sign of affection they gave him. He had the real Scotsman's kindliness of heart, and to kindliness of heart the Indian will invariably respond.

* * * * *

After four days' marching through the fairly level valley the path began to ascend towards the ridge which separates Kangra from Kulu. And now the real joys of travel were to commence. For the way now lay through forest—true, wild virgin forest. The cultivated lands, the hedges, the walls, the enclosures of all kinds were left behind, and I was in a forest where I could move as I chose and where all was wild and natural. To a child a real "wild" flower has a fascination which no garden product can ever exert. And to a man a real "wild" forest has the same attraction. And this forest I was entering was truly wild. It is nowadays becoming more and more eaten into: but it is the same which extends from Kashmir through Kangra, Kulu, Simla, and so on right down the Himalaya to Sikkim and Bhutan.

Like all good things, it is possible to have too much even of a forest. African travellers have found this. And Mr. James and I were to find this two years later in Manchuria. The first plunge into a forest is always delightful. But if for weeks together you can see nothing but forest and hardly see the sky, and have never any outlook, you weary of the forest as you never weary even of the desert. You feel cramped and oppressed. You feel as in a cage, and long to push aside the trees and get some breadth of outlook. In this Kangra forest there was, however, none of this oppression. I was not shut in. From many a knoll and spur or opening in the forest I could get far distant views over the valley itself—over the first ripples of the rising Himalaya, each ripple a deeper and deeper purple as it shaded off towards the plains of India, and all telling of distance, colour, warmth and mystery. Or, on the other hand, I could look upward towards the great Himalayan range and see its glistening snowy summits rising close at hand above the trees. I had no sense of confinement whatever. And the serene, intense blue sky could everywhere be seen above and between the trees. The air was neither too hot nor too cold, neither exhausting nor chilling, but just delightfully inebriating. And the noise of splashing water added the last touch to the exuberant effect.

And the water alone was worth the journey. In India water is regarded with profound suspicion. It is the fertile carrier of disease and death. Only at the risk of life do we ever drink it pure. We filter it and boil it or drink it in its aerated artificial forms. Usually it is drawn from dark, deep, unwholesome wells. In big towns where there is a proper water-supply it reaches us through hidden pipes as it does in England—pure perhaps, but with all the life and sparkle gone. But here in this mountain, in the forest, in the open air, in the dazzling sunshine, tossed about among the boulders, dashing from some rocky height, resting in some sequestered pool, what a wholly different thing it was! With no half-fear disease would follow, but convinced that fresh life would come, I could lie flat down by the edge of a stream, and with my face on the running water gulp down mouthful after mouthful; and standing up again, refreshed and thankful, feel that I had just enjoyed one more of the real good things in life.

Then, reinvigorated after the long pull up the mountain path, I could sit on a rock and just enjoy the forest. And this, too, I could do without fear or annoyance. The rocks and forest were dry, not soaking wet as farther down about Darjiling. And there were no horrible leeches or vexatious mosquitoes. There was nothing to annoy me. I could rest after my walk and drink in every delight with no disturbing thought and feel that life was good.

And I never now in England, nor in Scotland, see a pine-tree top against a deep blue sky, or smell the fragrance of the pines on a dry summer day, without thinking of this Himalayan forest. For this forest was mainly of pines and firs and spruces, and where I stood, mostly of the stately deodar.

There was nothing like the wealth of plant and insect life there is at the same altitude in the Sikkim Himalaya—no semi-tropical vegetation—no tree-ferns, no orchids, no vibrating hum of insect life, and nothing like the same number of butterflies. And of what there was of plant and bird and insect life I observed but little. For, as I have said, what tendencies I had had to study natural history had been left undeveloped. And, besides, my mind was now thrown far forward to great mountains still farther on that I wanted to reach. I was marching from twenty to twenty-five miles a day in order to see them. And I paused far too little to enjoy the country I was actually passing through at the moment.

Still, ignoramus as I was in all that concerned natural history, there were a few things I could not help observing, and hurried as I was I could not but enjoy them. First there were the deodars. This forest was the home of the deodar cedar, and all who have been to Simla know its beauty. It is akin to the Cedars of Lebanon, and I have seen a very old deodar in Kashmir, growing quite alone, which spread out its branches far and wide very like the Lebanon tree as we see it in an English garden. But in the forest the deodar has not room to expand, so it grows straight and stately, but with those gracefully turned-up boughs like the corners of a pagoda roof. It is a tree very dear to Englishmen in India, bringing with it memories of many a glorious "leave" from sweltering plains and dark depression to a cool hill-station and a cheery life.

But most conspicuous at this season were the

crimson rhododendrons—not mere shrubs, but regular trees growing like huge flowers in among the pines and cedars, and lighting up the dark green forest with their glowing red. Often they were so closely intermingled with the cedars as to make it seem as if the deep red blossoms were springing from the deodars themselves. These rhododendrons (*R. arboreum*, grown now in England) are in bloom along the Himalaya at this time of year from Kangra right down to Sikkim, the great home of the rhododendrons, where grow also mauve and white and yellow coloured species; and if only one could fly along the Himalaya like a bird, what a lovely band of colour in the greens below the snows this rhododendron stretch would show!

The ferns were other objects which even I could scarcely help observing. These again were not so large or so varied as those ferns of Sikkim, which can hardly be surpassed, growing as they do in a hothouse atmosphere with constant moisture. But there were graceful maidenhairs, and for airy grace and lightness the maidenhair anywhere is very hard to beat. And the sight of these clustering round the edges of some sparkling waterfall, and ever freshened by its spray, was enough to wipe away for ever the remembrance of the scorching heat and dust of India. And besides ferns on the ground there were strings and festoons of the most graceful creepers climbing up the trees and suspended from bough to bough. And in addition to the pines and rhododendrons there were such familiar English trees as horse-chestnuts, sycamores and maples.

The forest held, therefore, many a delight for an exiled Englishman. And I could enjoy it all the more because I was not visiting it for a few hours in a day, but was living in it all day long, and day after day. And I was in splendid health and at the top of my bent. The world to me seemed good and I enjoyed it.

* * * * *

And, as I was trudging happily along through this entrancing forest, I suddenly saw an unusual sight—an Indian dressed in yellow of peculiar hue. Curious to know exactly who he was, I resorted to the freemasonry of the road and asked him. He said he belonged to the Salvation Army—at that time still struggling into existence even in England. He had already converted 117 people, and, though he had walked thirty-three miles that day, he had still energy left to try and make me number 118 on his list. He did not succeed: but be did impress me. And of all forms of Christianity I rather think that the Salvation Army form is best adapted for appealing to the masses in India. In its emotional appeal, in its dead earnestness, in its unwavering conviction, and in its loving solicitude for the souls of individuals, it touches the hearts of Indians: and the good the Salvation Army has done in India in the nearly forty years since I met this yellow-apparelled man in the Kangra forest is incalculable.

* * * *

My first pass I crossed on May 6. It was the Babu Pass, separating Kangra from Kulu, and was only a little over 10,000 feet in height.

But it is the first pass I ever crossed in the Himalaya, and is therefore held by me in respect. As I intended to make a double march that day so as to reach Sultanpur, the capital of Kulu, I started before sunrise. The path followed up the course of a little mountain torrent which came tossing down from the pass in a succession of waterfalls, generally arched over by the forest trees. Near the summit a little of the winter snow was still remaining—the first I had seen since I left England, and exciting me almost as much as it excited my retriever, who scampered about and rolled in it and barked and jumped in huge delight. Then came the thrill of reaching the actual top and seeing "the other side." Nothing extraordinarily grand was disclosed. But extreme grandeur I had not expected. I did, however, look down into the beautiful wooded Kulu Valley, and across to a new snowy range of, anyhow, more than Swiss Alpine altitude. Rhododendrons were growing even at the top of the pass, and the path on the other side led through magnificent forest, and for some distance over snow. The air had a real cold nip in it. Coolies I met were huddling together to keep themselves warm. And to keep myself warm I ran down the far side through the forest, and by ten reached Sultanpur, which is only 4,000 feet above sea-level, and therefore quite hot in the middle of the day.

Here I was to make my preparations for ascending the Beas—the river on which Sultanpur is situated, and one of the "five" rivers of the Punjab —to its source in the Rotang Pass, 13,000 feet high; and for crossing that pass into Lahoul, a country wholly different in character from Kangra and Kulu, and in which I hoped I might have glimpses of some true mountain giants. Here at Sultanpur I had the good fortune to find Mr. and Mrs. Dane. He was now Assistant-Commissioner and practically king of Kulu, and he afterwards became Foreign Secretary of the Government of India, and then Lieutenant-Governor of the Punjab. And Mrs. Dane, who was a niece of Sir Henry Norman, I had known since childhood. I had therefore a cheery afternoon and evening with them and received plenty of help and advice. Of all the many posts he held in India there was none Sir Louis Dane really *enjoyed* more than this in Kulu. He is a born engineer and would have risen to perhaps even higher eminence in the engineering profession than he did in civil administration. And to tour about Kulu, Lahoul and Spiti at his own sweet will, and to all intents and purposes entirely his own master, was a highly congenial occupation. He could and did plan roads, make roads, plan bridges, make bridges, open up new routes, foster trade, encourage cultivation, stimulate tea planting and fruit growing, and generally develop this lovely country hidden snugly away from over-much official attention, but needing just that enthusiastic personal care which Louis Dane was so prepared to give it.

And in this favoured valley the people are as charming as their wooded mountains. They are not grave and sedate like the people of the plains. They are bright and cheerful. Laughter is often on their lips. They love adorning themselves with flowers. And any kind of "tamasha"—singing, dancing, music—they enjoy like children. They have never been, so far as I know, a warlike race or very ambitious. And I have never heard of Kulu soldiers distinguishing themselves. But they are a happy, contented, prosperous people, and only ask to be left in peace to cultivate their fields. And the women are so good-looking, cheerful and attractive that two or three of the English settlers in the valley have married Kulu women and permanently settled down in Kulu.

Thus charming was the valley through which I was now to march. And my preparations did not take long, for the whole of my baggage weighed only eighty pounds, including tent, stores and bedding, and my servant I was leaving behind in case he could not stand the cold and might hamper my movements. All I wanted to do was to make a dash into Lahoul and back, just to have a glimpse of what the country was like on the far side of that wall of the Himalaya—for the Rotang Pass was across the actual main line of the Himalayan range. So I did not stop a single day at Sultanpur, but hurried off the next morning with a couple of coolies carrying my kit.

I see in my notes that passing through the bazaar I noticed a fine Kulu blanket, and that I bought it for six rupees—about half a sovereign. Never was a better bargain. It was of thick homespun wool and twelve feet long, so could be doubled up. That blanket I had with me on all my Himalayan journeys. And I have it to this day.

It looks out of its element in a trim English bedroom, so it is pensioned off and allowed to pass its closing days in a remote cupboard. But I like to visit it now and then and with gratitude recall the many nights it has kept me snug and warm when outside all was gripped in frost.

The road lay along the river's edge, and I was astonished to find the water icy cold. The air was very hot, for the valley was low and narrow and the sun was powerful. But the river, being fed by the melting snow and glaciers of the higher mountains, was both cold and very muddy.

At every level place were encampments of traders waiting for the Rotang Pass to be clear of snow so that they could cross into Lahoul, and proceed thence to Ladak, and some, perhaps, even to Yarkand. I looked on them with curiosity, for these were men who really did know the Himalaya and were wont to venture even to Central Asia. They were tanned and hardy men, not over-clean, but genial and polite and ready to talk, living in small tents with a large coloured flag over each, and with their goods neatly piled up in the centre of each encampment. They enlarged on the length of the journey to Yarkand, the number of passes to be climbed, the "poison air" on the highest, the uninhabited character of the country, the deep rivers that had to be crossed, and the number of ponies that died on the way. Yet they seemed cheerful enough at the prospect, and I daresay looked forward to the profits they would make from exchanging the cotton-goods from India for the charas (hemp drug), felts and carpets from

Turkestan—and also to the joys of Turkestan, where food and fruits are cheap and life comfortable. While travelling they seemed to live chiefly on a mixture of brick tea, clarified butter, salt and barley meal. Their goods were carried on the strong, rough ponies I afterwards came to know so well—patient, sure-footed beasts which are capable of enduring incredible hardships. They also had with them numbers of sheep and goats, which they kept both for the milk and the wool, which they themselves spun and wove into garments. And ponies, sheep, and goats alike were allowed to wander about at will, for all would answer at once —or nearly at once—when called. The mountains, the men, and the animals all seemed extraordinarily close to each other. The men knew the mountains and the animals, and the animals knew the men. There was a homeliness between them, and it seemed as if none would be very happy without the others.

And belonging to the Kulu Valley itself I saw many animals—large flocks of sheep and goats—being driven down to Sultanpur, where some would be sold, though most, after their wool had been shorn and sold, would be used to carry back grain to the higher villages of Kulu and Lahoul.

* * * * *

My first night I put up with a tea planter, whom I always think of as "old" Mr. Mennikin, though I daresay he was not more than thirty, for in those days I used to look upon anyone over thirty as far gone in age. He was a true aristocrat—an aristocrat,.that is to say, in his own particular line, which was tea-growing. He was not the servant of a company. He grew his own tea, and he grew, not for the multitude, but for the few. He cared not a rap whether he made money or not, and I suspect he made very little. But he loved growing just a little of the very best, and selling it to those who really could appreciate good quality. These were Russians, who would pay him twenty shillings for a pound of his best tea.

Most of the day he used to spend seated in a tree watching his tea bushes and keeping an eye on the coolies. And as the leaves began to shoot, he would himself go round, picking off the most delicate young shoots and personally supervising the withering and drying. I am afraid this must have been thirsty work, for at six o'clock in the morning he woke me offering me a glass of whisky, observing that "a wee drop in the morning was better than none all day." And I daresay this may have been perfectly true, but I observed that he himself had a good many drops at other times of the day besides the morning, so he was not very good testimony. Anyhow, no one could have been more hospitable or more kindly in giving me a help along the road.

* * * * *

Ascending steadily and passing gradually out of the cultivated part of the valley with its bright fields and apple orchards, I arrived on May 8 at Bashist, and was now in the midst of typical Alpine scenery, with snowy mountains rising on either side, and in front of me, at the head of the valley, a massive mountain 20,000 feet in height. The mountain-sides were everywhere covered with pine forests, and pines grew even out of the steep cliffs on any little projecting piece of rock, and magnificent waterfalls fell from the mountain heights. Such scenery is, of course, not at all uncommon. But its being common does not detract from its beauty. And I felt something growing and expanding within me as I dwelt on one or other feature of the scene. I really had reached something worth coming to see. I had not reached the grandest Himalayan regions. But to look on that vast forest of stately pines, to feel myself braced against those strong, rugged precipices, purified by the example of those snowy heights, and calmed by the clear blue sky overarching all, was an experience I would on no account have missed. I delightedly drank it all in, and let it sink deeper and deeper within me. It was for this that I had come, and great satisfaction filled me.

But more still had I to see, and the next day I set out for Rala, at the foot of the Rotang Pass. And now flowers came more in evidence. As the forest opens out at the higher altitudes there are little meadows of flowers. And to my amazement I came across a man bringing back a sack-load of white violets, while farther on I saw a mass of them laid out in the sun to dry. It seems that they make some kind of liquor or medicine out of violets. What I noted as purple cowslips, which I presume were primulas, I also saw, as well as anemones and flowers looking very like primroses. But the sight of these did not thrill me to anything like the same extent as the sight of the River Beas cutting its way through sheer rock and forming a chasm two or three hundred feet deep, crossed by a bridge only twenty yards long. The sides of this chasm were perfectly perpendicular, and of clean hard rock. And at the bottom the river was foaming and tossing with tremendous force and impetus. It gave the impression of an irresistible force meeting an immovable body, and finding a solution of the problem by cutting its way clean through the body. The body did not budge, but was simply cut in two. For such an operation unlimited time is, however, required. And for, perhaps, some thousands of centuries that river may have been at work.

* * * * *

The next day, May 10, the second anniversary of my obtaining my commission, was the crucial day of the whole trip. For on it I crossed the actual range—the main range of the Himalaya, the direct continuation of the same range in which Mount Everest stands, and which is a continuation of the Alps in Switzerland. It was a great day for me. It was also very disappointing. For weeks I had had visions of this pass as a desperate climb along knife-edge ridges, or along the face of frowning precipices, with a drop of thousands of feet into a foaming torrent on the one side and perpendicular cliffs on the other. Instead, I had first a dull grind up a steep hill-side for a mile or two, and then nothing but dull plodding through soft snow for all the rest of the way to Kokser on the far side. I had, too, from one cause and another a splitting headache all the time after I had entered the snow, and a feeling of lassitude and depression.

Though I was not aware of it at the time, I was, of course, suffering from mountain-sickness. The pass, though not a high one as Himalayan passes go, was over 13,000 feet above sea-level. And when you are first at that height, and when you are walking and not riding, and when you are walking through snow and not on hard ground, and when the sun is beating down on you as if it meant to penetrate right inside your aching head, and when the glare upward from the snow is almost as bad as the sun itself, and when in addition to everything else there is a piercing wind blowing and bitingly cold, you do feel sickness of some kind or other, whether it's mountain or not. You begin to wonder what on earth induced you to come to such a place, and only your pride keeps you still plodding on.

So I kept on at it, feeling ever more miserable the higher I ascended. At length I reached a fairly level stretch. Ahead was a wide expanse of dazzling snow, and above this, straight in front of me and apparently rising from it, was a jagged line of rock with spiky peaks, and over this, I took it, I had to climb. This I imagined was the pass. It did not look so very far distant—three or four miles—and I could make out almost all the details. So preparing for this as my final struggle I persevered on. When all of a sudden—to my astonishment—I came to a point where the snowy expanse suddenly dipped downward: and there deep below me was the narrow valley of the Chenab River, and that ridge of spiky peaks I had thought was the pass was really the range on the far side of the Chenab. I was, in fact, already on the summit of the Rotang Pass, and my climb was over. But the air in that region was so exceedingly clear that the range, ten or twelve miles off, had appeared to be only three or four miles away, and to be directly connected with the snow of the pass.

It was a relief to find I had no more climbing, and I ran down the snow on the far side to get to warmer levels as soon as possible. But on the whole I was disappointed. I felt a sense of disillusionment. I had counted so much on this view from the top of the pass; and I found not very much in it. When you are already at 13,000 feet, a 20,000-feet peak does not look especially high. And there seemed to me a depressing desolation all round. There was hardly a sign of life anywhere. The forest line had been passed—and once over the line of the Himalayan range there is seldom any forest, even at fairly low altitudes. The clouds have spent themselves on the Indian side, and little rain or snow falls on the far side: so the mountains on the far side are bare. The whole scene was depressing in comparison with what I had expected. And perhaps this was inevitable. The actual seldom comes up to our expectations. We form for ourselves pictures of what we expect to see, and those pictures are always in glowing colours and of most exquisite forms. And the actual when we see it is but a sorry figure in comparison. Yet the actual may not be quite so bad as it appears. Perhaps the fault lies in some part with us. Perhaps, fter all, there is a great deal more in it than we see at first sight. It may not correspond exactly to our anticipations. But we ourselves may be blind to the excellences it really does possess. And Lahoul may after all not be so depressing and gloomy as it appeared to me that day.

And what makes me think this may be so, and that the fault lay with me and not with Lahoul that I felt so cheated and disillusioned, is that only a few months later when I was travelling along the edge of the Afghan frontier and met the Lieutenant-Governor of the Punjab—Sir Charles Aitcheson—and Lady Aitcheson on tour, and I remarked to them how dreadfully barren and ugly the country was—nothing but bare brown hills—they expostulated vehemently, saying that the colouring on the hills in the mornings and evenings was simply heavenly. And when I came to look at the country the next day from their point of view, I saw an astonishing degree of beauty I had not seen before. I had not indeed previously been looking for beauty. I was out on a military reconnaissance and my mind was intent only on military requirements. I was thinking of how the mountains could be defended or attacked, and what passes lay across them, and what supplies they furnished. And I had thrown out the remark about their being ugly without much thought. I had, of course, in a casual way noticed their beauty at dawn and sunset. But I should never have realised how great a beauty there was if it had not been pointed out to me, and if I had not seen how much others appreciated and enjoyed it And in the same way in the case of Lahoul, I have not the slightest doubt that, if I had had the eyes to see it, there was beauty enough to satisfy all my longings.

But if it is the case that we are almost invariably disappointed in the actuality when we have keenly looked forward to it and built up hopes about it—if it is true that the beauty of a scene never quite comes up to our expectations of it, it is equally true that in retrospect, in looking back, we are never disappointed. We have been struck speechless with the beauty of some scene. We have treasured it for years in our minds, and we have half feared that when at last we are about to see it again it will not really be as beautiful as it has been all these years in our memory. But yet when the great moment arrives, and we actually see it once more, it is far more beautiful than our remembrance of it! There is never disillusionment over the beauty of the past—over beauties we have seen. I have scores of instances in my mind at the moment—Kinchinjunga, Nanga Parbat, the autumn in Kashmir, and a lot of others. And every Englishman who has returned to England on a summer day knows of this. Through all his exile he has treasured up the remembrance of a summer day in England. He paints beauty after beauty in his mind. But when he actually sees it he finds he has never pictured it half beautiful enough. If he is disillusioned at all, it is in finding how little he had remembered how beautiful England actually is. Or, to take a commoner instance still, every winter we picture to ourselves the glories of the spring. We bear in remembrance some perfect day in spring and our enjoyment of it. But when winter is at last over and a spring day really comes, who is ever disappointed in it? Who ever has said, even to himself, that it does not come up to his expectations, and that he had remembered it as something better still? We know full well that we are never disillusioned about the beauties of the past. And if often, or even always, the beauty of an object we see for the first time is not up to the picture we had made of it with our imagination, we need not be depressed. The particular kind of beauty that we had expected may not be there; but there may be beauties of many another kind, if we would use our eyes to see them.

Such, indeed, proved to be the case in Lahoul. I arrived worn and cold at the Rest House in the bottom of the valley, on the bank of the roaring Chenab, and I found it icy and comfortless. It had been under snow all the winter, and the snow was now melting and lying about sloshy and chilling. A fire seemed to have no effect in warming the cold, damp room. All the heat went up the chimney. I was badly wanting a good, filling, comforting hot meal, but I had cut my baggage down so narrowly that all I could get was a cup of Liebig, some chupatties (native bread), kippered herrings, and tinned beef, and this in only half the quantity I wanted. I could not stop in that wretched room. But outside it seemed little better. There was no sign of life and vegetation except for an occasional bird. Huge depressing mountains shut me in on every side, and the whole valley looked, so I say in my notes, "inexpressibly dreary and desolate."

Then came the surprise. And what I saw then was, as I also remark in my notes, "worth while coming all this distance with my eyes shut to have seen." After my frugal dinner I had been strolling disconsolately about outside having a look at the stars before turning into bed, when I noticed that towards the east it was getting lighter and lighter, just as if the sun was rising behind the mountains, only the light was white and silvery instead of ruddy. Lighter and lighter it grew. Peak after peak was lit in the silvery radiance. At last the moon at its full appeared above the mountains, and the valley was almost as light as day. For the air at this height and on the far side of the great wall range is clear like crystal; the snowy whiteness of the mountains reflected back the moon's white rays. And all now being again in the hard grip of frost, mountain and valley alike were glistening and sparkling in the silvery light, and what had only just before appeared the very desolation of desolation was now transformed into a scene like fairyland. Not only the dreariness but the solidity of the mountains seemed to have disappeared. They seemed unsubstantial as a dream, and glowing with a radiance not of earth. This was one of those rare and unexpected treats which come when all that one really had expected has proved a disappointment.

* * * * *

I stopped one day in Lahoul to visit the Kokser village—a miserable closed-in collection of houses. Then I hurried back to Kulu. The ascent from Lahoul back to the top of the Rotang Pass was fearfully steep and very slippery. And when I reached the top I found clouds were collecting, and by the time I reached Rala rain was falling. But after a meal I pressed on again through the rain for another march to Bashist; and the next day I again double-marched, twenty-four miles, to Sultanpur, and was at last in warmth and in something like civilisation, with plenty of food.

I had had my little fling. I had caught just a glimpse of the other side of the Himalayan range. But I thirsted for more mountain beauty, and on my way from Kulu to Simla I hoped to be able to make a detour up the Sutlej and get a sight of the gorges by which it has cut its way through the Himalaya. So I started off from Sultanpur along the Simla road again walking two stages a day that I might get in all I could. After the upper Kulu Valley the country was dull. I marched through cultivated lands and past numerous prosperous villages, at length reaching Rampur by a steep descent. Here I was to have crossed the river, but the bridge was closed on account of some infectious disease on the other side, and my plan for reaching the gorges was balked.

It was a disappointment, for from what I had heard these gorges must be some of the finest in the Himalaya, and great gorges are extraordinarily impressive sights. But if I could not go there I could at least dream. And as I looked up the Sutlej Valley to where they must have been, and towards Tibet, from which the river flows and in which it takes its rise, I dreamed of a journey to that mysterious country. I would pierce through the Himalaya, come out on the highlands of Tibet, see marvellous mountains, visit the great lakes, explore the sources of the Indus, the Sutlej, and the Brahmaputra, come to know the curious people of that secluded country, make a great name for myself, and be known ever after as a famous traveller. This was the ambition I formed now, and after turning it well over in my mind I wrote to the Secretary of the Royal Geographical Society for advice, and I still have Mr. Bates' reply.

* * * * *

All that, however, was for a future year. For the present I had to turn towards Simla. And the first march back was dreadful. Rampur is a most picturesque little town, with the temples and the better-class houses built of deodar cedar, richly carved and in style much like the Swiss chalets with wide overhanging roofs. But it is situated right down at the bottom of the Sutlej Valley, only 3,000 feet above sea-level, and at the end of May was extremely hot. I had to climb from it 3,000 feet on to a ridge before I descended again to the bridge by which I should be able to cross the Sutlej, and I felt little inclined to make the climb. There was nothing to look forward to to act as a spur to my lagging spirit. I was not making for any goal. I was, indeed, turning my back upon what had been my goal, and was making down instead of up the Sutlej. The air of this shut-in valley was stifling, and the sun beat down on me with suffocating force. I felt utterly listless and disinclined to face the hill. Nevertheless, it had to be faced, so I determined to make my mind a blank and turn myself into a pure machine. I would think neither of the heat, nor of where I had to get to, nor of future schemes. I would not even look up to where I had to go. I would simply look on the ground and watch my feet going tramp, tramp, mechanically upward. The plan answered splendidly. After a time I did look up, fully expecting to see the top of the ridge miles beyond me yet; but to my astonishment there it was close at hand. The air was cool. I was well out of the valley, and very soon I was in a fairly clean and comfortable dak bungalow.

Next day I had to descend on the other side of the ridge to the Sutlej again. And crossing the river I had a less painful ascent, much of it through woods, and eventually reached Narkanda. This is only four marches from Simla, and is well known to those who seek a change there from the work or gaiety of India's summer capital. But though well known it is none the less beautiful, and is one of the choicest spots in all the Himalaya, for it is 8,000 feet above sea-level, and therefore cool and refreshing in the hot weather. It is set on a ridge amidst forest surroundings, and has commanding views over the Sutlej Valley to the main Himalayan range on the far side, with its everlasting snows and rugged peaks of 20,000 feet in height. The air here was delicious, and the sun not too hot; and I could lie under the pine-trees in cool and comfort, and dream and plan to my heart's content.

I spent here an afternoon and evening of rare delight, and then pressed on to Simla and Kasauli, to civilisation and the society of my countrymen and countrywomen, for the last fortnight of my leave. And there what was bound in the nature of things to happen befell me, and Kasauli holds for me sweeter memories than any other spot in all the Himalaya.

* * * * *

My trip was now over. I had had a glorious holiday. And when I returned to my regiment in the frightful heat of July, before the rains had broken, I was too full of future plans to think much of the heat. I was fairly launched on my career as a traveller.

CHAPTER III

TURKESTAN TO INDIA

When your heart is full set upon an object it is curious to note how one circumstance after another arises to help in its achievement. Obstacles innumerable, of course, also are met with. But not obstacles alone. Many favourable opportunities arise which, if seized and made the most of, all go to the accomplishment of the end in view. Certainly I was wonderfully fortunate. Opportunity after opportunity came to me.

Scarcely had the cold weather commenced than I was sent for one day to the orderly room, when the Colonel asked me if I would care to join a reconnaissance party which was being sent to report on the passages across the Indus from the frontier. It was explained to me that the Divisional Staff had asked that the regiment should supply a senior officer to take charge of the reconnaissance, and he would be assisted by a junior officer from one of the infantry regiments. But the senior officers in the regiment were not particularly interested in reconnaissance and knew little about surveying, and the Colonel, knowing that I was keen on surveying and reconnaissance, thought I would be the most suitable officer to send. I, of course, jumped at the opportunity. It was a splendid chance, and gave me work after my own heart. And I remembered how the Surveying Instructor at Sandhurst, Captain Kitchener, had told us cadets that surveying was a good thing to take up, as it generally led to something good. He instanced his brother Herbert in the Engineers, who had taken up surveying and was now (1881) doing very well in Egypt.

No sooner had I returned to my regiment at Rawal Pindi from the reconnaissance than the Divisional Staff again asked for me. This was early in 1885. The Russians were moving towards Merv. The Amir of Afghanistan had been invited by the Viceroy, Lord Dufferin, to meet him at Rawal Pindi. And an army of 20,000 men was to be concentrated there to impress him, and to be in readiness for a forward move to the frontier or into Afghanistan should war with Russia eventuate. And my humble services were called in by the Quartermaster-General's Department, under which I had been serving during the reconnaissance, to aid in fixing sites for camps, receiving regiments and directing them to their allotted camping ground. And when all the Headquarter Staff arrived I came to a certain extent under their notice.

This was my second piece of luck. My third came in May of the same year. The Intelligence Department at Simla asked the Divisional General at Rawal Pindi to send an officer from that Division to Simla for the hot weather to undertake the revision of the Military Gazetteer of Kashmir. The Divisional Staff thought that I would be a suitable officer for the task. The result was that by the middle of May I found myself comfortably established in a room by myself in the Military Offices at Simla, with every book and report on Kashmir at my disposal, and, in addition, a certain amount of information not vouchsafed to the public about the present position of the Russians in Central Asia.

This was, indeed, a chance. I doubt whether I did much good with that Gazetteer, and I have never dared ask for it since. I read through all the books and reports, and amassed enormous numbers of sheets of notes from them. But whether this undigested material was ever of the slightest use in directing the military affairs of the Indian Empire I should very much doubt. What I did do, however, was in my spare time to study the general position of the Russians in Asia. I came to the conclusion that they must eventually make a movement in the direction of Manchuria. And having come to that conclusion, I proceeded to look up all the information I could find about that country, and compile a résumé of that information. And this led to important results—important, that is to say, as far as my own personal activities were concerned. For I soon found that very little indeed was known about Manchuria. From what little information there was available it was evidently a country of great possibilities, with immense forests in one part and rich fertile cultivated lands in other parts. But it had never been thoroughly explored, and it was consequently a promising field for a military explorer.

Throughout those months at Simla I must have been a singularly unsociable person, for I thought and talked and wrote of nothing else but travel. I looked out for anyone I could travel with. I tried to get some newspaper to employ me, and in every possible way I strove to get off on a journey. The result of this was my fourth and chief piece of luck, and that was meeting Mr. H. E. M. James (afterwards Sir Evan James). He was then Director-General of the Post Office in India, and was contemplating making a journey into Chinese Turkestan and Tibet with his friend Mr. Carey. Both through Robert Shaw's journeys and also through my work on the Kashmir Gazetteer, I was able to give him a deal of information about the routes he might have to follow, and without a thought of joining them was deeply interested in all their plans. The sequel was that a few weeks later Mr. James appeared at my house and asked me whether I would go a journey with him in the following year, 1886. He had not been able to get his leave in time to join Carey, so had now to make separate plans. I could have jumped with excitement. Here was the very chance I had been longing for. I accepted at once, and went about Simla all that afternoon brimming over with pride, and looking with compassion on all the wretched people around me who were doomed to be plodding on in their offices or drilling with their regiments, while very soon I should be out in the wilds seeing all kinds of wonderful country and having many xciting adventures.

Where we were to go had not yet been decided. But gradually we came round to Manchuria. I had my précis of information about Manchuria, and I thought I should be able to get sent there officially, or be allowed special leave to go there, if I could show I could bring back military information of value. Mr. James had also been recommended Manchuria from another source—I think Mr. Archibald Colquhoun. So eventually we decided that Manchuria should be our objective.

I returned to my righteously grumbling regiment in October, and in March, 1886, set off with Mr. James for Manchuria. We spent seven months in exploring the country, and the result of these explorations is given in Mr. James' book, "The Long White Mountain." An abbreviated account of it I have also given in my "The Heart of a Continent." I will not, therefore, say more about it here. All I want to say is that this Manchurian journey brought me to Peking, and that it was from distant Peking that I set out on that journey to India which necessitated my traversing the Himalaya from the one side to the other in their entire breadth. And it is this exploration of the Himalaya with which I am concerned in this book.

Before, however, I describe my adventures in the Himalaya and the wonderful sights I saw there, I must say just a few words about the journey which brought me to Yarkand and to the northern approaches of the great mountain range. After our Manchurian journey Mr. James returned to England by America, while I proceeded to Peking, where I spent the winter in the British Legation, intending to return to India by sea in the spring. But towards the end of March, Colonel Mark Bell, V.C., the head of the Intelligence Department in India, under whom I had been serving at Simla, arrived at Peking with the intention of travelling across China and Chinese Turkestan to India. And I immediately asked him to take me with him. This proposal he declined, on the ground that it was waste of effort for two officers to travel over the same ground. But he suggested that while he went by the regular road through the populated parts of China proper, so as to gain all the military information possible, I should find my way by the unknown route across the Gobi Desert. This suited me even better, and I nearly burst with excitement at the prospect.

And indeed this was a big enterprise I was to embark on. Since the time of Marco Polo, six centuries before, no European had travelled from China to Central Asia. And even at Peking, the capital of the Chinese Empire, it was difficult to get information about the outlying parts. I could get no information about the route across the desert of Gobi, nor about the present political condition of Chinese Turkestan. And I was still only twenty-four years of age when I set out with two Chinamen (one of whom refused to go any farther when he arrived at the desert) to find my way to India, about 3,500 miles away.

This has been a long preliminary to show how it came about that I made my first exploration of the himalaya from the side of Central Asia and not from India, and that instead of making for Yarkand from India, I made for India from Yarkand.

I arrived at Yarkand on August 29, and there had to set to work forthwith on preparations for the last and severest stage of my journey from Peking to India. When I had left Peking I had anticipated proceeding to India by the ordinary caravan routes across the Himalaya by the Karakoram Pass and Leh. This was the route followed by Robert Shaw on his three journeys to Yarkand, and is the regular means of communication between India and Turkestan. It crosses high passes, and the traders suffer great hardships from cold and wind and the rarefaction of the air. Still, it is used every year, and it was this way by which I had thought I should reach India.

But as I entered Yarkand I was handed a letter from Colonel Bell, written from the Karakoram Pass, and suggesting to me that instead of following his footsteps along the well-known route I should strike out a new line and explore the route to India by the Mustagh Pass, leading into Baltistan and thence to Kashmir. From my work on the Kashmir Gazetteer I knew of this pass. It is marked on many old maps. And it was evidently at one time a recognised route between Baltistan and India. But no European had ever traversed it, and we had no information about it even from native sources. I found, indeed, from enquiries at Yarkand that no native had crossed it for twenty-five years. It lay across the main watershed between India and Central Asia—across the range which divides the Indian from the Chinese Empire. It would certainly be very high and probably very difficult. And close by it on the range it crossed was a galaxy of peaks second only in altitude to the Mount Everest group—one of them, K_2, being only 724 feet lower than Mount Everest itself.

I was thrilled with the prospect of such an exploration. I had no mountaineering experience. I had no mountaineering appliances. I had not even enough money, and the only pair of boots I had left was a nailless pair of "town" boots bought in a store at Peking. Still, I never doubted that I should get through somehow or other—"muddle through," as we like to call it in England. And whatever I didn't have, what I certainly did have was the enthusiastic help of all the Indian traders in Yarkand. My very youth was on my side. With the trustfulness of youth, I had placed myself entirely in their hands, and they at once formed themselves into a committee and took charge of me completely. They were a cheery, genial lot, very solemn, dignified, and deferential when they came to pay me a formal call, but gay and light-hearted as boys when they took me out to an orchard and entertained me to dinner—a dinner in the open and commencing with a dessert of melons, grapes and peaches plucked in the garden itself. Some of them were Indians who had come to trade in Turkestan. Some of them were natives of Bokhara and Kashgar who were accustomed to trade with India. All therefore had known what hardship is, and all had sympathy with a traveller. And they set about my preparations with a will.

First they found me a guide—a man who had actually crossed the Mustagh Pass, though it was twenty-five years before. And a splendid guide he proved. When he was first brought before me he seemed callous and indifferent. He said he knew the way and would show it to me, but only on condition that I trusted him. He had heard that Englishmen trusted their maps and not their guides, and if I was going to trust my map I might, but he would not go with me as guide—what was the use? If, however, I would trust him, he would undertake to land me in Baltistan, which was his native country. I took to Wali immediately. I had no scruple in assuring him I would not look at a map—because there was no map to look at. The country I should pass through in the vicinity of the great watershed was entirely unexplored. And Wali looked a hardy, dependable man who would be likely to make good his promises. He was taken on accordingly, and joined the conclave which were making the preparations.

For the control of the whole caravan there was fortunately at hand a first-rate man, Mohamed Esa, who seventeen years afterwards accompanied me to Lhasa, and was lent by me to Sven Hedin for his last journey into Tibet. Mohamed Esa was a native of Ladak and originally a Buddhist, and from travelling frequently to Yarkand and mixing so much with Mohamedans he had espoused Islam. He was a man of great hardihood. He could endure cold and blizzards and privations better than any man I met in the Himalaya, and cover longer distances. In after years I employed him on many occasions when endurance was required, and he never failed me. Where he would have failed, but where I never tried him, was where courage rather than endurance was required. He would stand up against Nature, but he quailed before his fellow-men. He would run no risks from the raiders on the Yarkand road. And when the fighting commenced in Tibet he unostentatiously withdrew to where he would be least likely to be noticed either by friend or foe.

This, however, was his only failing, and for running a caravan he could not be surpassed. He was always cheerful and always quick, ready and resourceful. He knew what those Yarkandi ponies employed on the trade route could do, and he knew what the men could do. And he could get the most out of both.

Under him was another Ladakhi, dear old Shukar Ali, the most happy-go-lucky Mark Tapley I ever came across. Never, under any circumstances whatever, did I see him anything else but cheerful. In fact, the harder things went, the more cheerful did he become. He had not sufficient authority for the leadership of a caravan. But for keeping the caravan in good spirits and for readiness to turn his hand to any nasty bit of work that had to be done—such, for example, as carrying me, of his own free offer, on his back across a glacier stream with huge blocks of ice swirling round him—he could not be beaten. Years after, when I was Resident in Kashmir, he came down from Ladak to see me, and kissed my feet and jumped up and laughed with delight, then kissed my feet again and behaved exactly like a dear big faithful dog who has caught sight of his master again after a long separation. And I loved him as men love their dogs, knowing that their fidelity can be counted on through every circumstance whatever.

Another first-rate man the committee produced was a Balti named Turgan, who had been captured by Kanjuti (Hunza) raiders and sold into slavery in Yarkand. The committee recommended me to purchase his release and take him back to his native country. I paid, I think, eighty rupees for him—seven or eight pounds—and got full value for my money. He also came across the mountains to see me when I was Resident in Kashmir twenty years later; and when I presented him to the Maharaja His Highness was gracious enough to excuse him and his family and his heirs for ever from the customary forced labour which stands in those remote parts in lieu of taxes.

Besides him three other Baltis settled in Yarkand were to carry loads if it should be found impossible to take ponies over the pass. And thirteen ponies were bought, and four Ladakhis (including Shukar Ali) were engaged to look after them.

Then the equipment had to be looked after. The men were provided with heavy sheepskin coats, fur caps, and new foot-gear. New pack-saddles and blankets and three sets of shoes were provided for the ponies. Big cooking-pots and a huge urn for tea were bought for the lot of us, as we would all feed together. And as for myself, most of my European clothes being worn out, I attired myself entirely in Yarkandi clothes, with the exception of my sun-helmet, which the committee advised me to wear in order to show I was an Englishman. So I had a long loose robe with long loose sleeves. And to sleep in at night when it got really cold I had a sheepskin sleeping-bag made up.

As for supplies, the committee sent on orders to Kugiar, the last big place, to have ready there three weeks' supplies for men and ponies. For the men (including myself) small dough cakes of flour mixed with ghi (clarified butter) were baked into a biscuit-like consistency, and besides this, rice, tea, sugar, and ghi were taken, and several sheep to be driven along and eaten one by one. And for the ponies barley was carried.

All this involved a greater expenditure of money than I had calculated upon having to incur when leaving Peking. But again the committee came to my aid, and offered to lend me what money I required simply on my writing an order. Years after I was given back the actual order I wrote. It was no regular cheque, but was written on half a sheet of ordinary notepaper. Yet this was quite sufficient for these kindly and confiding traders. And that they should have trusted me like this is testimony to the good name my predecessors had established.

When all these preparations were completed the committee had up the men, and fervently enjoined upon them to behave well and see me safely over the Mustagh Pass to India; and, accompanied for a mile or two on the way by a number of these kindly, helpful Central Asian traders, I left

Yarkand on September 8. I was not yet in sight of the mountains, for the air was heavy with the depressing dust haze which hangs almost perpetually over Chinese Turkestan, and which is due to the dust blown up from the desert. And my first night's halting-place gave little indication of the hardships I would have to endure, for I put up in a fruit garden, and my bed was on a platform with a kind of lattice-work roof from which hung a profusion of grapes, so that I had only to reach up my hand to pick as many as I wanted whenever I liked.

But in a few days we plunged into the mountains, and leaving Kugiar, the last place at which we could obtain supplies, we crossed first a pass of about 10,000 feet and then the Kuen-lun range—a kind of outer barrier of the Himalaya—by the Chiragh-saldi Pass, over 16,000 feet in height. And now real business commenced, and the thrill of the adventure began to steal upon us. We had passed all human habitations, and there were no paths. Ahead of us I could see a regular maze of snowy peaks. And through this we should have to find our way.

And we had to be on guard, too, against the attack of Kanjuti raiders. These were wont to issue from the deep-set, secluded valley of Hunza and raid both the villages of Turkestan and the caravans on the regular Karakoram Pass route to India. Three of my men had themselves been captured by these raiders, so they were able to speak from experience. In consequence we slept in the open behind rocks, for fear a tent might attract attention, and for fear, also, lest we might be caught at a disadvantage inside one. And I, of course, always had my revolver ready.

The Yarkand River was reached the day after crossing the pass, and from there onward I was covering entirely new ground. Hayward had descended the Yarkand River from its source as far as this, but beyond this point no European had ever penetrated. I was now really plunging into the unknown. And a few days later we felt the real thrill of exploration and the true tussle beginning. We had built up a path through some fearful gorges in the Yarkand River, and had ascended a tributary stream towards a range which I named the Aghil range and bivouacked a few miles from its summit when Wali, the guide, said he could not recollect the way ahead.

We had had an exhausting day scrambling through the minor gorges of the tributaries. We had forced our way up the stream itself, through icy water, and amidst boulders covered with ice. We ourselves were drenched through. And the poor ponies had cut themselves about most terribly on the slippery rocks. But they had faced the ordeal in the most gallant fashion, for nothing seemed to daunt these hardy Yarkandi ponies. And the men, too, had behaved magnificently, Wali showing the general line of advance and he and I doing the reconnoitring on ahead, while Mohamed Esa superintended the progress of the ponies. And all had lent a hand in bad places, removing boulders, building up some semblance of a path, shoving and hauling the ponies, unloading them if necessary, and carrying the loads on to a more favourable part.

Now we were through the confined part, and were high up on comparatively open ground, where there was a certain amount of rough scrub for the sheep and ponies to nibble at, though no trees or bushes, for the mountain-sides were quite bare. Ahead of us, like an impenetrable rock barrier, without a chink through which we could creep, rose the summit ridge of the Aghil range. And here we halted in the afternoon on some fairly soft level ground, unloaded the ponies, and prepared our bivouac, while Wali gathered together his recollections and prepared for the venture on the morrow.

Now!—now, at last—I was to see all that I had dreamed of three years ago in Robert Shaw's house in Kangra, on my first trip in the Himalaya. Now I was on the verge of the very inmost core of the Himalaya and would see its most splendid sights. The strain of the great adventure was sensibly tightening on me. And as it came I braced myself to meet it. And real life began to tingle through my veins.

While the ponies were being fed and the Chinaman was cooking our evening meal, and Mohamed Esa was looking after the gear and the men were enjoying their smokes, I strolled about peering into that barrier in front. It was formidable enough in appearance, and Wali for the moment had forgotten the way. But I was confident he would find a way through. But what lay on the other side?—that was the mystery. This was only the outer barrier. What would the main range itself—the line of the highest peaks, the great watershed between Southern and Central Asia—be like? That was what I tried to imagine.

And then I came back to my party. The sun had now set behind the mountains. The chill of sundown began to steal over all. The little streamlets became coated over with ice, the air being crisper and sharper. But there was no wind and no damp, and we settled cosily round the fire and had our evening meal together. And by now we had shaken down into a compact and cheery party. The elements were incongruous. Ladakhis from Leh, Baltis from Baltistan, a Chinaman from Peking, and an Englishman from an island at the other end of the earth. But we were all together on a big adventure. We were all in first-rate health. We were seated round a blazing fire. There was plenty of good warm stuff in the pot in front of us. And the stars were twinkling brightly above. All ate heartily. The inevitable tea was handed round from the vessel which acted as tea-pot and tea-kettle combined. Then tongues began to wag. Wali tried to rake up his memories of twenty-five years before. He was sure there was a gap in the barrier somewhere: but whether to the right or left he could not remember. Turgan discussed the chances of a band of Kanjuti raiders coming upon us, for we were right on the track they followed. Mohamed Esa told stories of the Karakoram. Good old Shukar Ali would corroborate each point with his cheerful, jolly laugh. And Liu-san would smile and chuckle away and put in a word or two in broken pidgin-English to show he was well satisfied with life.

When we had eaten as much as we wanted—and there was no stinting, for, knowing that men who have to work hard and endure much must be well fed, I had told the committee they must arrange for ample supplies—we prepared to turn in. We did not intend to sleep where we were, round the fire, which would have been the most comfortable thing to do, for fear some lurking Hunza raider might have seen us. But when it was quite dark—or rather as dark as it can be in those starlit regions—we removed ourselves away from the fire behind rocks where we thought we should be safer. Then the men curled themselves up in their sheepskin coats; and I crept into my sheepskin bag and settled down comfortably for the night.

√Not that it was easy to go to sleep straight off. Healthily tired as I was after the day's exertions, I was too excited to sleep at once. And lying on the ground in my nice warm bag, with my staunch companions about me, I looked up at the fairy mountains round me, at the steel-blue sky above, and at those glittering stars I had known so well in the desert, and I thought to myself *this*—this really is living. Now I really am alive. Now I really am doing something worth doing. Deep, splendid inner satisfaction came upon me. And gradually I sank off to sleep.

* * * * *

As soon as light began to break we were astir next morning. It was freezing hard. What had been a running stream was frozen solid. A good warm breakfast, with plenty of hot tea, was soon ready for us all. The ponies were fed and loaded up, Shukar Ali shouting cheerily all the time. And then we started off, making straight for the mountain barrier, which was about five miles distant, covered with snow wherever snow could lie, but presenting mostly an appearance of rugged, precipitous cliffs.

I marched eagerly on ahead with Wali, both of us anxious to solve as quickly as possible the problem as to how we could surmount the barrier. Wali said he knew we should have to turn sharply either to the right or to the left, but which it was he could not say for certain. Happily, as we got close under the range all doubt disappeared. A wide valley opened up on the left. Wali recognised it at once, and said that up it we should find the gap we were looking for. I could restrain myself no longer, but pushed on ahead even of Wali. We could not actually see the pass, but there it undoubtedly would be. And on the other side—what?

The going was perfectly easy. The valley was wide and open. And I walked on as hard as I could. But the pass seemed positively to recede as I advanced. As I topped one rise I would find there were other rises beyond. And, eager as I was, my pace began to slacken just when I was wanting it to increase. For I was at 16,000 feet above sea-level, and at that height you cannot walk at any rapid pace. At last I came to a little lake; beyond it was a rise I was sure must be the pass itself. I worked myself up for a final effort, and literally ran up the rise. And this one really was the top. And beyond? What did I see there?

Beyond was the fulfilment of every dream I had had three years ago. There, arrayed before me across a valley, was a glistening line of splendid peaks, all radiant in the sunshine, their summits white with purest snow, their flanks stupendous cliffs. And bearing away the rich abundance of their snowy covering were vast glaciers rolling to the valley bottom. I lay down on the ground and gazed and gazed upon the scene, muttering to myself deep thankfulness that to me it had been to see such glory. Here was no disappointment—no trace of disillusionment. What I had so ardently longed to see was now spread out before me. Where I had reached no white man had ever reached before. And there before me were peaks of 26,000 feet, and in one case 28,000 feet in height, rising above a valley bottom only 12,000 feet above sea-level. For mountain majesty and sheer sublimity that scene is hardly to be excelled. And, austere though it was, it did not repel—it just enthralled me. This world was more wonderful far than I had ever known before. And I seemed to grow greater myself from the mere fact of having seen it. Having once seen that, how could I ever be little again? That was the kind of feeling this mighty scene produced.

And then, too, the thought came on me: How strange it is that so few men should ever see this grandeur! Century after century, for thousands and thousands, perhaps millions, of years, those mountains have stood there in all their radiant glory. But how wasted was it, with no human eye to see it! And perhaps it is because of this that we who have been privileged to see such sights have a peculiar longing in us to be able to communicate to our fellows something of that glory we have known.

* * * * *

It was an hour before the caravan caught me up, and then I had to bring myself back from dreams and think of what we had to do. The mountains ahead of us were very grand and very magnificent, but the practical point to be considered was how we were to get over them. How that was to be done did not seem particularly clear. But first we had to get down to the valley of the Oprang River, which ran at the base of these stupendous mountains and flowed down from some vast glaciers we could see in the distance on the left. So we descended from the pass and soon found a good patch of jungle at which to bivouac for the night. And the next day we ascended a tributary of the Oprang—a tributary which ran directly down from the great range—and again we bivouacked in some good jungle, though it proved to be our last comfortable bivouac where we could have plenty of firewood before the tussle with the mountains began in earnest.

But before the struggle actually began I had one of those surprises which make up for every hardship. Ever since I had begun to think about the Himalaya, I had wanted to see at quite close quarters some stupendous snowy peak. Now, all of a sudden, as we rounded a corner, I saw, up a side valley on the left, a real monarch which threw utterly into the shade my uncle's picture of "A Peak in the Kuen-lun." It towered thousands of feet above me, and quite close by; and it was one of those sights which make you literally gasp as you suddenly see them. My whole being seemed to come to a standstill, and then to go rushing out in a kind of joyous wonder. I kept saying to myself, "How simply splendid! how splendid!" There before me was a peak of almost perfect proportion, clothed in a glittering mantle of pure white snow and ice for thousands of feet, and standing up head and shoulders above all the mountains round, though they themselves must have been of the order of 20,000 feet above sea-level. The sight of that tremendous mountain, so massive, so firm and strong, so lofty, and so spotlessly and dazzlingly pure and white, necessarily left an impression which has lasted through life. It could not fail to do that. But it did something more; it provided a measure and standard in my mind by which I tested things. This has its inconveniences, for when you have in your mind a standard so lofty and so pure, you feel miserable at not being able to come up to it. But anyhow, you have seen what real loftiness and purity is, and are able to appreciate it when you see it. And this is something for which you can never be too thankful.

CHAPTER IV

THE MUSTAGH PASS

PERHAPS it is well that we only have short glimpses of these greatest sights of all. I had had to descend rapidly from the Aghil Pass, and so lose sight of that bright array of icy peaks. And soon we had to round another corner and lose sight of this mighty peak, which I assumed at the time must be K_2, 28,278 feet in height, though whether it actually was I am unable definitely to say. And now we advanced up the valley, at the head of which Wali assured us was the Mustagh Pass. All around us now were great snow mountains, and though from this distance—about twenty miles—we could see no gap in them, Wali was confident he could find a way.

As usual, I walked on ahead of the caravan, and after two or three miles found the whole valley blocked from one side to the other by what appeared to be huge mounds of broken stones and rocky débris. And on reaching them I was astounded to find they were mounds of solid ice, and that it was only the surface that was covered with these rocky fragments. They were, in fact, the extremity of a glacier—the glacier which flows down from the Mustagh Pass. But I had never seen a glacier before, and had no true idea of what a glacier was like. I had imagined the ice might be a dozen or score or two of feet in thickness at the most. And I had always pictured the glacier with the ice all visible on the surface; but here no ice was visible. The surface from one side of the valley to the other was all rocky moraine. And the ice, instead of being a score, was a couple of hundred feet or more in thickness.

This is what I saw as I first approached the glacier. And when I ascended one of the mounds I was dismayed to see that they extended for what might have been nearly twenty miles right up to the main range, gradually merging into the whiteness of the snow and ice. I was completely taken aback. Here was something I had never counted on. And I thought it would be quite impossible to take ponies up it, and that they would have to be sent back. It seems ludicrous that I, who had never seen a glacier in my life, should be exploring the greatest mountain glacier region in the world—and should be exploring it with ponies for transport. But so it was. And it was fortunate, therefore, that I had with me such willing and experienced men.

For on returning from my short venture up the glacier, I found Mohamed Esa and Shukar Ali gallantly leading the ponies up the glacier as if it was all in the day's work—Mohamed Esa going about in a business-like way, showing the men leading the ponies where to go and how to help them; and Shukar Ali, in huge delight, shouting, "Khabar dar! Khabar dar!" (Take care! Take care!), and "Kuch parwa ne" (Never mind).

While I had never thought for a moment that ponies could be got up, they had never thought for a moment that they couldn't. So on we went. And my spirits rose as I saw such a buoyant spirit in my men.

The glacier itself, too, as I came to look into it, was a gorgeous sight. What I took to be walls of hard rock, when I came close to them turned out to be walls of transparent dark-green ice; and there were the most fantastic caverns, with floor, walls, and roof, all of ice, and with delicate icicles hanging from the roof and fringing the entrance. It was an entrancing sight to a novice like myself, and again I felt that I really was seeing what I had so often dreamed of. But for the ponies it was a different matter; they, poor things, were having a dreadful time. The coating of débris on the surface of the glacier being only very thin, they would kick it away as they scrambled up the side of a mound, and would slip on the ice beneath and cut themselves about most terribly. Exertion at these high altitudes was also very exhausting. But we had plenty of men, and shoving and hauling the ponies we helped them along, and so progressed up the glacier.

Next day we came to a point where even the men could not see a way ahead, and they turned to me and asked me to have a try. Perhaps by my "iqbal" (good fortune) I might find one. I tried my luck. With a couple of men I went back down the glacier, then found a way on to the middle of it—on to what is called a medial moraine—followed it up, and found there really was a possibility of getting the ponies along. And having satisfied myself about this, we set off back again. But it was nearly dark now. We lost our way, and for a time had a dreadful fear we might have to spend the night on the glacier without food, fire, or warm clothing. At last, however, we hit off our party, had a warm meal, and turned in pretty well exhausted after the long day's work.

Our third day on the glacier was easier. We got the ponies on the line we had reconnoitred, and in the evening bivouacked at the head of the glacier not far distant from the summit of the range. But in the evening the two men we had sent at earliest dawn to reconnoitre the pass itself, and see how far it was practicable, returned to say that it was quite impracticable for ponies, and would be difficult even for men.

This was serious news, for we were now at the very climax of our venture. What should we do now? Wali said the only thing to do was to try the old Mustagh Pass. What the men had reconnoitred was the "new" Mustagh Pass on our right. But there was another, older pass, on our left, which it might be possible to get men over. We would try and get over that and reach Askoli, the first village on the Indian side—the village from which Wali himself had come twenty-five years before—and from there send back supplies to enable the men who could not get over the pass to proceed with the ponies to Shahidula, 180 miles distant, and right round by the Karakoram Pass to Leh. This was all we could do; and even that might not be possible: even men might not be able to get over the pass.

We had an anxious conference that night as we sat round the fire, eating the evening meal of rice and mutton which Liu-san had cooked for us. Wali was grave, but determined. He had undertaken to see me through. And see me through he would. Mohamed Esa and Shukar Ali were cheerful and ready, but did not realise what they might be in for. Liu-san was as imperturbable as ever. He had followed me faithfully from Peking, the capital of the Chinese Empire, and he was now within a couple of miles of its extreme western limit. We had together overcome a good many obstacles, and he supposed we should overcome this one. So, as he had always done before, he just did his own work well, and trusted to me for the rest. And for myself, I simply took it for granted we would get over—just as when I rode out of the Legation gates at Peking, on this long journey of very nearly four thousand miles to India, I took it for granted I should get there all right, somehow or other. Difficulties, dangers, hardships, I reckoned on. But the thought of failure never crossed my mind. It was not that I had to suggest it. It simply did not arise. Quite unconsciously I counted on my capacity to meet and overcome the difficulties as they arose. What they would be, what would be the means of overcoming them, I could not say beforehand. But what I was convinced of was, that when they arose and the strain came on me, I should find myself rising to the occasion and discovering means of overcoming them. A man can do a great deal more when a crisis is on him than he can calculate upon in cold blood. And that is why I so firmly disbelieve in cold calculations. Of all misleading things they are the most misleading though they have the superior air of loftiest wisdom.

All the same, I felt graver that night than I did on the night at the foot of the Aghil range. The difficulties were undoubtedly greater than I had expected. The severe exertions of the last few days and the altitude—about 18,000 feet—were beginning to tell. And we had to economise fuel, so could not have a roaring camp fire, as we had had every night till we got on to the glacier, but could only have sufficient wood to cook by. The cold was also greater. For we were now high up amidst nothing else but snow and ice. The great mountains rose white on every side, and close by was the actual ridge we should have to cross upon the morrow. And as we laid ourselves down upon the glacier the cold seemed to come streaming down from the icy peaks, and to take a grip on us and all about us. Not a breath of air was stirring; all was absolutely still. But the cold itself appeared to be in motion and gripping tighter all it touched, freezing up every little streamlet brought to being by the sun, and creeping about us, too, till we had covered ourselves cosily up for the night. Though then, with our bodies warm and in repose, came the great peace of the stars, which glistened so steadfastly on us as we slept on the face of the glacier.

• • • • •

Before daybreak the next morning, September 28, Wali roused us all. My moustache was clamped tightly to my beard by my frozen breath, and all below my nose was a mass of ice. It was fearfully cold, and the temperature must have been well below zero. But we soon had some hot tea and some bread, and then we started off, leaving Liu-san and a few men behind with the ponies, and only taking just sufficient food to carry us to Askoli, three or four days' march away. We took no tent, of course. But I took my fur sleeping-bag, and the men their sheepskin coats. Our cooking equipment consisted of one large tea-kettle. And for food we took the dough biscuits we had had cooked in Yarkand, and some tea and a bottle of brandy—the whole forming one coolie load.

The ascent to the pass was only severe on account of the difficulty in breathing. It was snow all the way, and not particularly steep. But it took us six hours to reach the top, for at 18,000 and 19,000 feet trudging through soft snow one quickly becomes out of breath. We could only proceed for a dozen or twenty steps at a time, and would then lean over on our alpenstocks and puff and pant as if we had been running hard. And keen as I was to see the top of the pass, there was no possibility of pushing on as I had at the Aghil Pass; I could only drag wearily along with the rest.

At noon we reached the summit. And then came the shock. There was no easy snow-slope down the far side. There was an almost sheer drop. I felt pulled right up on myself. It did not seem possible to get down such a place. The only chance was to traverse an ice-slope on to a cliff which jutted out through all the snow and ice. But that cliff itself looked dreadful. And I thought we were done. But I did not say so. For I wanted to know what the men thought of it. I was without experience of mountain climbing, and this might be something not much out of the ordinary which no true mountaineer would think a great deal of. I would not give myself away before the men, but looked at it with an air of we would, of course, proceed down.

From what I saw afterwards, I rather gather that what was passing in my mind was also passing in my men's. They probably were also thinking it would be impossible to get down, but did not like to give themselves away before me. As so often happens in such cases, everyone is afraid in the bottom of his heart, but no one likes to show how afraid he is. So each emulates what he thinks is better in others than in himself. And in this case there were two deciding factors. Wali was a man of stern principle. He felt strongly the obligation to see me over the range. And he meant to carry out the obligation. And this was entirely a freely formed obligation on his own part. I had neither put a revolver to his head in the approved melodrama fashion and told him that unless he showed me over I would shoot him, nor had I offered any pecuniary advantage such as giving him so much more if he got me over and so much less if he failed. A sum had been fixed at Yarkand by the committee, and that sum he was to get in any case. But the motive which was now actuating Wali was neither fear of a bullet nor greed of gain. It was simply the need of satisfying his own high sense of honour. This was the first factor.

The second was my own self-pride. I was now at the very climax of my whole long journey. I was actually standing on the exact dividing line between China and India—between the waters that flow to India and the waters that flow to Central Asia. If I could get down that precipice the last great obstacle would be overcome; the way down to Kashmir and India would be clear before me; and I would have traversed a route from Turkestan to India which no white man had ever seen before. If I failed to get down, I should have to go back a whole long way, and arrive in India with the ignominy of failure. Success was in sight. I could see the glacier below. I shuddered at the look of the precipice. But the incentive to risk it was tremendous. And at the back of all was the confidence that somehow or other the thing would be done.

So Wali and I looked at each other, and without saying a word he commenced making preparations for the descent. No order by me was given. No order from me was asked. We were all of us men who meant business, and we proceeded to our business. We had no Alpine appliances of any kind. But I had read that Alpine climbers tied themselves together on a rope. So I had a rope made of the spare ponies' ropes that we had brought with us. Then I had read that Alpine climbers cut steps in the ice, so we had brought a pickaxe with us, which Wali was to use as he led the party on the ice-slope. We none of us had nailed boots. My last pair of European boots had been cut to pieces on the glacier, so, like the men, I had only leather heelless native boots—more of the nature of leather stockings than boots with soles and heels.

Thus equipped we set out for the slope, Wali leading, I following him, and then Shukar Ali, Turgan (the released slave), another Balti, and Mohamed Esa. The slope was of hard ice, and a little below us ended in a sheer ice-fall on to the glacier below. Wali cut steps with his pickaxe, and we followed in the steps he had made, steadying ourselves as best we could with our alpenstocks—stout sticks made in Yarkand with a metal point to them. But now we were actually on the slope, the dreadful thought occurred to me that if one of us slipped he would carry the rest with him in one death-plunge into the icy abyss below. Being tied together was a positive danger. The rope would have been of advantage if each member of the party had had a regular ice-axe by which he could anchor himself to the ice-slope. But the alpenstocks we had formed no sort of an anchor. And what added to our risks was that the noonday sun beating on the ice-slope melted the steps which Wali cut and made them most dangerously slippery, and our smooth native boots with the water became quite slimy. Even the handkerchief I tied round did not add much to the security.

I was in a state of cold, horrible fear, which was

not lessened by Turgan kicking fragments of ice from the slope to watch them hop down and then disappear over the edge into the abyss. But I was made still worse by Mohamed Esa from the end of the rope saying he could face it no longer and must go back. I had looked to him as next to Wali my great stand-by, and up to now he had been most dependable. But he was shaking so with fear he was almost a danger to us. So I told him to go back and look after the ponies.

The slope was crossed at last, and we found ourselves on a firm, solid rock, which for the time was a relief. But the prospect ahead was appalling. The getting down the precipice looked worse than crossing the ice-slope. Fear colder than ever came over me. But Wali seemed now more in his element. He did not mind the rocks so much as the ice, and he proceeded to lead the way down, discarding the rope, which I, too, was thankful to have done with. The dreadful part was that we had to let ourselves down, step by step, on to rocks which were by no means secure. We had neither firm foot-hold nor firm hand-hold. With great trepidation I would lower my foot, feeling for some firm hold; but now and then, as I gradually let my weight come on it, it would give way. And even when I had found firm foot-hold, I feared to let my hand go. One slip of hand or foot and all was over.

Poor Mohamed Esa had summoned up courage to come across the ice-slope after all and join us on the precipice. But only for a few steps. Then he utterly collapsed. He said he could not stand it any longer, and salaaming profusely to me, a little way down by now, said he really must go back. This was for me the very tensest moment of all. But I dared not show my feelings. And I braced myself up with the thought of what other men had done in perhaps tighter places.

I am often asked now what is the good of climbing Mount Everest. And I say it is good as furnishing a standard of what can be done. At this critical point on the Mustagh Pass I called to my mind descriptions and pictures of what Alpine Club men had done in climbing the Alps. And I thought to myself that the men who had performed those feats would think nothing of this, so why should I be so fearful? So their climbing feats were of real practical use to me now. Then I thought of men shooting markhor and ibex. They must have to go over rough ground like this; and if they took it as a matter of course, why shouldn't I? And, curiously enough, I thought of the riding-school in my regiment, of being bucketed round and round with a lot of recruits on a rough horse, on a polished saddle with no stirrups, and the rough-rider sergeant giving the word Tro-o-o-t and then Ca-a-a-nter, and the pace getting faster and faster, and of my tightening my knees to the saddle as hard as ever I could, and trying to keep steady. And I thought of that sergeant himself as he showed the recruits how to ride—of his steady nerve and the nerve he put into the men. So I had in my mind a jumble of Alpine Club climbers, and men shooting markhor, and the rough-rider sergeant of the K.D.G.'s, and between them they managed to make me present a decent appearance before these Himalayan men I had with me. And Wali and all of them were as good as they could be. Often they would guide my foot as I lowered it on to some firm bit of rock and keep it steady there while I lowered my hands. And so we progressed down the precipice.

Then we came to a point where the rock ended and a further ice-slope began. But, fortunately, through the ice-slope at no great distance there protruded a good firm-looking rock. So we made up a rope of all the bits of rope we had, and on to this we tied all the men's turbans and waist-bands. Then we tied one end round a man's waist and let him down to the rock. On the way, with the pickaxe he cut steps in the ice-slope. And then, with him holding the improvised rope firmly at the lower station and we holding it firmly at the upper, Shukar Ali went down using the steps. Then I followed. Then Wali. Then came a Balti, who in coming down slipped and came headlong down the slope, but fortunately still held on with one hand. This hand was fearfully cut. But we managed to fetch him up on the rock, and then Wali, instead of commiserating with him, abused him roundly for being so stupid. And this was really much better for him, and for everybody, for it made him pull himself together. Here, indeed, Wali was acting on the same principle as riding-masters act on with recruits. A recruit is by no means commiserated with when he tumbles off. Far from it!

We were now all down except Turgan, the man

who had so little nerve as to enjoy watching ice-fragments tumbling over the edge of the ice-slope into the abyss. He would have the worst time of all. Our mode of procedure was this: he was to fasten his end of the rope round his waist, and then come down as best he could by the steps that had been cut. And if he slipped, we at the lower end would pull in the rope as fast as ever we could and haul him in. He might fall past us, but if the rope held we hoped to be able to check his fall and drag him up on to the rock. Luckily he did not slip. He came steadily down, and the whole party was assembled now on the island rock.

Two more stages of the ice-slope we descended in a similar way, letting ourselves down on to protruding rocks. Then the slope became easy enough for us to get down without cutting steps the whole way. And at last by sunset we reached the glacier at the foot of the pass and stood in safety once more.

The relief was tremendous. The last and greatest obstacle had been overcome. I was now in India, and my object had been achieved. With the tension off, deep, swelling gratitude came surging up within me—that deep, satisfying thankfulness a man feels when he finds he has fulfilled himself—has done the thing which he was built to do. That satisfaction in its full intensity can only be felt at the supreme moment of achievement. For once that moment is passed a man has to be thinking of more else to accomplish. But the satisfaction in all its fulness of intensity was on me, as with the light of the setting sun I took a last long look up at the Mustagh Pass and thought of the dangers we had passed and the victory we had won.

* * * * *

Wali had fulfilled his obligation. He had piloted me safely over the Mustagh Pass. I was now in India, in the territories of the Maharaja of Kashmir. And we would gladly have bivouacked where we were at the foot of the pass, for we had been on the move all day without a break. But there was no sign of either ground to lie on or of scrub for fuel. We were on the snow-field at the head of the glacier, and round us was nothing but ice. So we trudged on still farther. But now we were descending. And we were in the highest spirits. Shukar Ali, who on the precipice had for once been serious and silent, was singing and laughing once more. Turgan was excited at the prospect of soon getting back to his own home. Wali, though he still kept up his grave look, was evidently pleased and lightened in heart. And I plodded along, pleased to the topmost with myself, with my men, with the world, and with everything there was.

And it so chanced that the scene was in perfect accord with my feelings. It was like the scene on my first night in Lahoul, only even more beautiful. The moon was nearly full; the sky without a cloud; the air intensely clear. And around us was not a speck of any but the purest white. Under that silvery radiance, in that crystal air, the glistening glacier on which we walked and the snowy mountains round us all-seemed a phantom fairy world of stainless purity and light. And tense though the strain had been that day, and great the danger, what remains deepest embedded in my memory is not the horror of that dangerous pass, but the beauty of those moonlit mountains as we marched on through the night.

* * * * *

But we were far too careless. Our dangers were not yet over. We still had need of caution. I chanced to look back at the men following me, and found one was missing. We thereupon retraced our steps and found the Balti who had slipped on the ice-slope had had another accident, and fallen down a crevasse. We had been disgracefully negligent in walking over this treacherous ice without being roped together. Often the smooth surface was merely a brittle bridge across an icy chasm, and it might or might not give way under our weight. In this case the ice had been strong enough to bear us four leading men, but had given way under the last man, and he had fallen through. And our whole successful day might have ended in deserved disaster if it had not been that the crevasse was narrow and he had been wedged in by the load of my bedding which he was carrying.

We let down a rope and soon extracted him and placed him in front of me. But again misfortune occurred. As I was close up to the roll of bedding I detected a strong smell of brandy. My only bottle of brandy was broken. Lady Walsham, at Peking, had insisted on my taking at least two bottles. One I had drank in the Gobi Desert, the other I had reserved for the Himalaya. Now it was gone, and gone just when it was really needed. The roll containing my fur sleeping-bag, the food, and kettle had been thrown down the pass to save being carried, but evidently had not been softly enough packed.

By eleven o'clock that night we at length reached a little patch of ground clear of snow, and here we decided to halt, though even yet there was no sign of any scrub to serve as fuel. All we could do was to break up a couple of our alpenstocks and make a diminutive fire of them capable of heating up sufficient water for a cup of tea all round. And this, with some native biscuits, served as our evening meal. Then I got into my sleeping-bag, and the men huddled themselves together in their sheepskin coats, and I was soon off to sleep, for we had had a terribly long day. We had started before sunrise, and it was nearly midnight, and almost all the time we had been on the move, and for six hours under fearful strain. But it was a day in a lifetime. A day in which I had really lived. We are told to "live dangerously." And we are told to lead the "strenuous life." That day I had lived dangerously enough to satisfy a Nietzsche, and strenuously enough to satisfy any Roosevelt.

* * * * *

And for some days yet I had still to lead a strenuous life. For if we were out of danger, we had plenty of rough going ahead of us. We had to start the next morning without any tea or anything warm. But at ten o'clock, near where the glacier from the Mustagh Pass joined the mighty Baltoro glacier we came across an old hut, the remnant of the days when the Mustagh route was used. And from wood lying about we made up the first good fire we had had for some days now and cooked ourselves some food, though even now we could not have a good square satisfying meal, for it might be three days yet before we reached Askoli, so we had to be sparing of our food, having brought as little as possible with us so as to leave as much as we could for the men remaining on the north side of the pass. All we had, therefore, were a few mouthfuls of meat, some biscuits, and some tea. Then we set off down the glacier and soon reached the Baltoro glacier itself.

This Baltoro glacier, which had already been surveyed by Colonel Godwin Austen and has since been explored by several Europeans, notably by Sir Martin Conway's and the Duke of Abruzzi's expeditions, is one of the great glaciers of the world. It is thirty-six miles in length, two miles in width —a slowly, steadily moving river of ice—and perhaps about 300 feet in thickness where I now saw it, and for the rest of the way down mostly covered with greyish granite moraine.

But more remarkable than the glacier itself was the region through which it flowed. It was different, and almost more remarkable than any I had yet seen, and again my wildest dreams of mountain grandeur were faithfully fulfilled. If it were not so grand, I would call it fantastic. For there were giant mountains of every conceivable form and structure consistent with their granite composition. Great massive mountains like the Masherbrum, symmetrical cone-shaped peaks like Gusherbrum, spiky rock peaks, peaks of dazzling whiteness, towers, turrets, pinnacles, needles.

Rugged, sharp-edged, bold, majestic was every mountain there. In sheer precipices they rose above the glacier. Austerity, hard and stern, was this region's leading feature. Softness there was none. And no one who is soft could ever penetrate so far. Only to the hardiest do these mountains ever give admission.

So lofty, indeed, were the mountains, and so tremendous was their effect upon me, that for the time I felt overpowered by their majesty. I was exhausted by my long exertions. I was underfed. And I only longed to be clear of the mountains and out on the open with soft warm air to bathe in. I was in no state to enjoy their stern, exacting beauty. Nevertheless I was taking in that beauty. It was leaving its impress deep upon me. And later, when conditions were more suited, the picture on my soul developed like a picture on some photographic plate.

Just opposite us, when we reached the Baltoro glacier, and only twelve miles distant, was the great Masherbrum mountain, 25,660 feet in height —that is, about 13,000 feet above where we were standing, and mantled for quite 10,000 feet in glistening snow and ice. Then away to the left, eighteen miles distant, and forming the range from which the Baltoro glacier takes its rise, were the Gusherbrum peaks, over 26,000 feet in height. K_2 itself I could not see, for it was round a corner on my left. But many another peak I saw, and saw in the most favouring conditions, for the air was extraordinarily clear, the sky was cloudless and of intensest blue, and the brilliant sunshine sharpened every rocky feature and brightened snow and ice.

But for all that it was a weary march down the glacier. The moraine was of sharp, cruel, rocky fragments. My boots were worn through to the bare sole of my feet. I walked first on my heels, then on my toes, and often slipped on ice below the débris. Feet and knees and hands were bruised and sore. And I was very hungry. The only relief that day was that by evening we reached a clump of juniper-trees, and so could have as big a fire as we liked. Besides which, we were now down to less than 12,000 feet above sea-level, so had left the hard, stinging frost of the Mustagh.

Next morning we reached the end of the glacier, and here a nasty mishap befell me. A great stream, laden with blocks of ice continually falling off the glacier, came gushing out of its terminus. And this stream we had to cross, and it was more than waist-deep. It was an unpleasant prospect, and when the faithful, ever-ready Shukar Ali offered to carry me over on his back I could not help accepting. He sturdily faced the stream. But unfortunately it had an icy bottom. Shukar Ali slipped on the ice and fell backward in the water with me under him. And in his struggle to right himself he kept pressing me down. I was very nearly drowned, but both of us eventually managed to struggle to our feet and make our way to the opposite bank. Soaked to the skin in the icy water I felt completely numbed. The only thing to do was to walk on hard till we could find some shelter. And when we came upon a cave I took off my clothes—the only clothes I had with me—and got into my sleeping-bag while they were hung for an hour in the sun to dry. Poor Shukar Ali and the men had not even that comfort. But in some fashion or other they managed to get themselves fairly dry, and then we trudged on again, still through mountains of surpassing grandeur, but which I was far too tired to more than note.

That night—the third since we had left our ponies—we lay down in a cave, and the next day eventually did reach Askoli. But it was a long and dreary march, for my feet were terribly sore, and I could proceed but slowly. By midday we had the joyful sight of the green trees of the village, and in that clear atmosphere they looked so near I thought we should reach them in an hour. But on and on I wearily plodded, and it was not till four that afternoon that we were actually in the village—a village dirty in the extreme, but a real haven to have reached at last.

Famishing with hunger, our first necessity was food. And food in quantities was brought me, and in quantities I ate it, greasy and dirty though it was—mutton-stew, rice, and tea—down it went, more and more of it, till I thought I could never fill myself. And my men did the same. And now that hunger was appeased we began arrangements for sending supplies back to the men on the far side of the pass.

But the inhabitants were none too friendly. Wali was a native of Askoli, and it might have been thought that they would welcome him back after his twenty-five years' absence. The contrary was the case. And Wali told me that but for the presence of an Englishman they would have killed him. The reason was this. Mountain people everywhere are very secretive about their mountains. Through long ages they have been barriers of defence, and mountain people fear that if their mountain secrets are known ill may befall them. Hitherto they had been safe from the direction of Yarkand. But now, without a word of warning, an Englishman appears. And if an Englishman can come, Hunza raiders might also come. Wali was a traitor and should be killed. This was their view.

And Wali dared not stay a day among them after I had left, he said. He must come with me towards Kashmir and then return to Yarkand by Leh. But as long as I was with him he could hold his own. He was a man of standing and a man of character. Between us we got the village elders to collect supplies and men to go back over the Mustagh Pass, and by the following day we had started them off, plentifully supplied with ropes and long poles for tackling the pass.

CHAPTER V

THROUGH KASHMIR

I WOULD have started off the next day, too, to examine the "new" Mustagh Pass—the one which the two men had reconnoitred from the north and found impracticable. But I was so unwell from having eaten that greasy, dirty food in such quantities on the day before that I had to give myself a day's rest—the first I had had since entering the mountains. Besides, it was rather going against the grain to go back. I had crossed the main range and my face was set to India, and it was hard to bring myself to go back to the range again. But I could not feel completely satisfied in my mind about the Mustagh Pass till I had seen with my own eyes that the route by the western as well as by the eastern pass was as impracticable as the men had reported. So I got together a little party and furnished myself with a new pair of native boots, and after the day's rest started back.

We did not go up the Baltoro glacier again, but turned north up the Punmah glacier before we had reached the Baltoro. This glacier was not so big, but the scenery was almost as grand—as I know from a few notes I made. I wish I could recall it better. But I cannot. I could not get my heart into that little backward trip. My zest was gone. And when I am not working with zest I do not take impressions. All I can recall is a glacier descending much more steeply than the Baltoro and tremendous cliffs arising from it, and the men sacrificing a bullock to appease the spirits in the mountains.

And this sacrifice of the bullock—a bullock for which I paid—gave them great satisfaction. We all had a royal meal that night upon the sacrificed animal. There was plenty of wood about, so we could have a huge fire. And the men's spirits rose visibly as more and more of the animal disappeared down their throats. Baltis have a careworn, depressed look at first sight. But they are a gentle, likeable people, and whenever the care of feeding themselves is off their minds they brighten up and unloose their tongues.

And this propitiating of the spirits who dwell in the mountains must fulfil some need in the human race or it would not be so common as it is. In every mountain-country spirits—good and evil—are supposed to inhabit the mountains. And it is not surprising that spirits of a peculiarly powerful type should be supposed to inhabit these stupendous mountains round us.

For what do these hillmen find? They find that on the rare occasions on which hey venture into these high glacier regions something dreadful happens—something to cause them real dread of the mountains. As they venture higher they are seized by gripping cold; feelings of weakness and sickness come over them; without warning great blocks of ice and rock come hurtling down the mountain-sides; or terrific winds and snowstorms assail them. These are the experiences they have. And some mind or minds must be at work to bring about these dreadful happenings. The problem is, then, to know what precautionary measures can be taken to propitiate these minds, or spirits, so as to ensure safety to themselves. The hillmen cannot *see* these spirits, but they infer their presence from what happens. These simple people infer also that what would please themselves will please the spirits. They therefore provide them with a good meal.

We may smile at these simple folk. But are they altogether wrong in supposing that there are spiritual powers at work in the world? We Englishmen do not believe in the existence of gods and demons residing in the mountains—that is to say, gods and demons more or less human in form. But a great many Englishmen believe that one great, good spiritual power, and one great, evil spiritual power, are at work in the world and influencing their lives for good or ill. I myself at the time, in a letter to my father describing my crossing of the Mustagh Pass, said that without God's help I could never have got over in safety. I had not then thought things out, and I merely expressed the current belief in which I was brought up, that an invisible Spirit was watching me, guarding me from danger, and in some way guiding my footsteps and preventing me from making a false step. Similarly, British generals in their despatches during the war expressed the view that they were specially guided by God. So, if we do not believe in the existence of a multitude of gods, many believe in the existence of one guardian God—an invisible spiritual power more or less in the form of man on a glorified scale and dwelling in the skies.

And when we come to scientific men—hard-headed and sceptical though they be—we find that in the last resort they believe in the existence of spiritual powers. Down at bottom—or as far down as science has yet got—science finds that the happenings which so disturb the mountain folk are due to the activities of electrons in their innumerable groupings and groups and combinations of groupings; and that electrons themselves are fundamentally spiritual in character in that they act of themselves under the influence of other electrons and of the whole universe with which each single electron is inseparably connected. They have, indeed, been described as "mindlets," from their possessing the rudimentary characteristics of mind. When a rock tumbles down a mountain-side and crushes a man to death, the mountain people think that it has been hurled down by an invisible spiritual power; and though the scientific man thinks that the grouping of myriads of electrons which form the rock has been attracted by the grouping of myriads of myriads of electrons called the earth, he, no less than the mountain man, would attribute the fall of the rock to spiritual agency—namely, the agency of mutual attraction. And philosophers would say the same. Many of the leading philosophers of to-day say, indeed, that nothing exists except spirit. They would agree with primitive man that the whole world and everything of which she is composed, down to the hardest rock, is animated—albeit animated in different degrees of intensity, a rock not being animated to the same degree of intensity as a man is, and the ordinary man not being animated to the same degree of intensity as the poet or the saint.

So these mountain folk are right in thinking that spiritual powers are at work in the world. But fortunately these powers do not act capriciously as these mountain peoples suppose: they act according to law; and we learn by experience what those laws are, and working within them gain freedom to achieve our own ends.

Having sacrificed a bullock to the gods in the mountains and had a good meal the Baltis were now in excellent spirits, and we marched cheerily up the glacier, over rough ground, it is true, but with no special difficulty till on the third day out from Askoli we came to a camping-ground called Skinmang, and here we were brought to a standstill. The glacier flowing down from the "new" or western Mustagh Pass came steeply down in a maze of seracs to join the Punmah glacier. There was no obvious way through this jumble, and the mountain-side was too precipitous to climb. I therefore decided to proceed no farther. I have not the slightest doubt that if there had been the same urgent necessity to find a way as there was in the case of getting over the old Mustagh Pass we should have found one all right. But I was not out on a mountaineering expedition.

All that I wanted to make sure of was that there was no feasible trade route or military route by this way, which I would have overlooked if I had not gone thus far. And it was evident enough that neither a military expedition nor a trading caravan could cross into Baltistan by the western Mustagh Pass. Having ascertained this I thankfully turned my head once more towards Askoli and at last to India.

And on the same day—October 13—as we reached Askoli, the party that had been sent to the "old" Mustagh Pass returned. They were a fine lot of men. For in spite of injuries to three of them they had succeeded in reaching the party on the other side and handing them over the supplies we had sent. So Liu-san, Mohamed Esa, and the rest were enabled to reach Shahidula and thence proceed by the Karakoram Pass to Leh and India.

With my mind satisfied on this point I did not wait a day longer at Askoli, but on the 14th set out by double marches for Kashmir, descending the narrow, precipitous Braldu Valley—itself worth a visit on account of its rugged, rocky grandeur. And only a few miles out of Askoli I had one of those surprises men give each other at times. Wali I had always looked upon as possessed of nerves which nothing could shake. On the Mustagh Pass, both on the ice-slope and on the rocks, he had shown not a symptom of fear. But now that we had to cross a rope bridge over a chasm he was simply trembling with terror and absolutely refused to go over. It seemed to me incredible. A rope bridge is not a pleasant thing to have to cross. It is made up of birch twigs plaited together and consists of three ropes, one for each hand and one for the feet. It is suspended across the chasm with the river foaming and tossing a few hundred feet below. And the swaying of the bridge and the swirl of the water below is apt to discompose you. Still you have a good firm hold for each hand and an assured hold for the feet, and we had neither of these on the Mustagh Pass. The rope bridge did not affect me in the least, while—I hope unsuspected by my men—I had been in dreadful fear on the pass. But with Wali things were exactly reversed. He had not minded the pass but was overcome by the bridge. And it was only after long hesitation and with the support of a man in front and a man behind that we got him over. But once he was over he lighted up more cheerily than I had yet seen him and let the men chaff him to their full and give back to him all that he had given them on the pass.

So we proceeded merrily along. And when we got out of the precipitous Braldu Valley into the open Shigar Valley I was able to ride a pony and at last feel that the toil of the mountains was over. At last, also, I was able to enjoy the mountains. The load of weariness and responsibility was off me. The oppression of the mountains was removed. I was no longer under great physical and mental strain. And I was in splendid health, for I had plenty to eat, and the weather was perfect—brilliant sunshine all day long, and the air delightfully warm after the icy blasts of the Mustagh. So could sit on my pony and chew the cud of my experiences in the highest mountains—ruminate on all I had gone through and the glories I had seen, and feel their influence deepening in me.

And the Shigar Valley itself had no mean glories of its own. It is a broad, flat, open valley: but it is bounded on each side, and at head and at base by lofty mountains of the ruggedest type, culminating in needle peaks or covered with eternal snow. The sky above was of the clearest blue, and in this autumn season the valley was glowing in the brilliant colours of the numerous apricot-trees, which are its special feature. It was, indeed, the very best season of the year for travel in this country, for the apricot harvest had been gathered, and quantities of them, with grapes and walnuts, could be procured in every village at a very low price. I let the men buy as many as they liked, and they marched along by my side chewing the dried apricots, chaffing about all the dangers and difficulties we had encountered, and laughing and singing. Shukar Ali, especially, was in great form, and the very broadest smile never left his face from the first thing in the morning till the last thing at night. This really was something like living, they thought, and they enjoyed life to the full.

Shigar, the capital of Baltistan, was reached on October 17, and here I had to remain for three days to get money wherewith to pay the Baltis of Askoli for the supplies they had sent and for their services. It is a picturesque little place, with a castle on the banks of the Indus, which, even here, many hundreds of miles from the plains of India, was a big, broad, strong-flowing river. For me, also, it was the first point of communication with the outside world, as there was a crude kind of telegraph line by means of which I could telegraph to India, though only in Hindustani.

But the telegraph line meant an Indian telegraph clerk, and the Indian telegraph clerk meant a certain degree of civilisation. This Hindu clerk proved to be most hospitable and entertained me to dinner. In one way and another we spent many hours together, for I was thirsting for converse with any kind of civilised being. Not that I did not really much prefer my good and faithful Wali, Shukar Ali, and Turgan, but there are certain refinements of civilisation which one misses greatly when one does not have them. And the clerk was devoted to music. For hours he would play away to himself on a stringed instrument, more or less resembling our violin. I am no musician myself, but I was fascinated by watching this man—watching his soul coming out, and seeing quite clearly to what it was aspiring. I have no recollection whatever of what he was like. But his playing I remember as one of the occasions on which I have best seen into the soul of India. Intense yearning was the keynote. Of sweetness there was none. It was an impassioned longing for a higher spiritual state other and better than the present. And though the poor clerk most certainly must have enjoyed playing this music and seemed utterly to lose himself, taking not the slightest notice of me and wearing a look of wrapt absorption, yet he did not give the impression of joy. Rather did he seem consumed by the fire within him.

* * * * *

The Kashmir Governor of Ladak having by telegram kindly lent me the requisite money I again set out, and two marches beyond Skardu had to part with Turgan, for we had come to his native village. He was full of gratitude at parting. But gratitude did not end in words. He appeared again at our next day's camp with quantities of dried apricots for me and a feast for the men. And his gratitude did not end even there, for twenty years after, when I had returned to Kashmir as Resident, he came all the way down to Srinagar, over 200 miles, to see me. And it is cases like this, of simple intensity of feeling, that make one feel so deficient in comparison. Poor Turgan had suffered dreadful buffetings in life. Baltis have a hard task of it to get a living from the land. Only where it can be irrigated will it produce food crops, for the rainfall is scanty and the sun is hot. Mountain streams have, therefore, to be led along the mountain-sides and across the face of cliffs to some good piece of soil, and then the land has to be built up in level terraces to receive it. Food is thus only obtained by the hardest labour. So, like many other Baltis, Turgan had tried to better himself by crossing the great mountains to Yarkand, but had been captured, as I have related, by Hunza raiders on the way and been sold as a slave. He had known the adversities of life. He had endured terrible physical hardships. And in outward appearance he was as hard and tough as a mountain birch. But there, in the inner core of him, was all the time this tender disposition, which neither his hardships nor his hard fate had been able to subdue. Or was it, perhaps, that the very hardness of his lot had made him tender? It is difficult to say. But certainly there must have been something good in him to start with. And so I have found with many other Baltis with whom I have been brought in contact on these mountain expeditions.

There was Wali, for instance, with whom I had to part two days later on, as he turned off to Leh to return to Yarkand. He was a man of higher standing than Turgan and had led a prosperous life in Yarkand. But he had the same kind of gentle, sterling good in him. No one would expect Wali to make a good soldier, or a good trader, or a good clerk. He was just a homely cultivator. But he had in him what any man might be proud to have—dependability and loyalty to his work. Wali could be relied on. He relied on himself, and everyone relied on him. He was very self-contained, and, except at that rope bridge, always composed. Neither hardship nor danger had any effect upon him. And though he did not inspire affection in the way that poor Turgan and Shukar Ali did, and was much graver, he commanded respect from all, and it is to him I am indebted for getting over the Mustagh Pass.

* * * * *

With diminished party I reached Kargalik, and was now on the main trade route between Yarkand and India. And here I was again most hospitably entertained; this time by the Governor of Ladak, a fine type of Hindu gentleman, Pundit Rada Kishen Kaul. He got up a game of native polo for me in which we both joined, and then he gave me a wonderful Indian dinner, with curries of an altogether different type to any which I had hitherto known. He was a high-caste native of Kashmir, of the true old-fashioned type, exquisitely clean in his dress and habits, and with remarkable composure and grace of manner. Centuries of strict and rigid training have gone to make a man like that, up against whom the ordinary Englishman looks remarkably uncouth and rude. Such men may not have the vigour and robustness of Englishmen, and they are very inadaptable and hard to move out of the groove in which they have been brought up. But it is sad to think they are dying almost completely away with their suave and polished manners and correctitude unshakable. And sadder still is it that their sons, under the impact of Western civilisation, have lost faith in what their fathers believed in, and yet have not found faith in our own way of life. Years later Rada Kishen Kaul's own son told me of the distress he had suffered on this account, and told me also of his father's grief. A son's defection means a terrible break-up in an Indian home. And it is impossible not to sympathise with both father and son. But what one would wish is that the sons would, at any rate, not imitate our brusqueness of manner, but retain all of their fathers' reverence, courtliness, suavity, and dignity. For these are possessions of great value, and bound in the long run to come to their own.

* * * * *

Having had a delightful afternoon and evening with Pundit Rada Kishen Kaul, I renewed my journey the next day, passing through a very dull country of bare rounded hills—hills, that is, in comparison with what I had been seeing. And on the day after I had an extraordinary experience. Ahead of me I saw a white man, and thinking that of course he must be an Englishman, and consequently the first Englishman I would have seen for nearly seven months, I pushed my pony along as hard as he would go. No one who has not been for months without seeing any of his countrymen knows how eagerly his heart will go out at the sight of one. It does not matter who he may be. Just the fact that he is one's own countryman is enough. One wants to shake him hard by the hand, see his smile of welcome, hear one's own language again, tell him all about oneself, ask him all about himself. There seems to be just everything in common between us.

And so I advanced to this stranger with an eager smile on my face and looking forward to an endless talk. And I was, in fact, warmly received and spoken to in English. But after a couple of words it was easy to see he was not an Englishman. He was, indeed, of all unexpected nationalities, a Russian, and the original of the Russian in Rudyard Kipling's Kim at that. He told me that he had been spending some months in India and was on his way to Ladak. I was sadly disappointed at not finding an Englishman. Still, he was a European, and that was a great deal. It meant that there was much in common between us. And to talk in my own language again was in itself a blessing. But we could not stop long together and had to set off each his own way. But when I said good-bye he struck a theatrical attitude, saying, "We part here the pioneers of the East!" As I was just at the end of a journey extending all the way from Peking, while he was only one march over the first pass from Kashmir and was on a well-worn trade route, I thought there was not much of the pioneering on his side. He turned out afterwards to be a regular adventurer—in the worst sense of that noble word.

Proceeding on my way to India, on the following day I crossed my last pass—the Zoji-la. It was only 11,400 feet in height, and quite easy on the approach from the north, though steep on the south. And now there was a sudden and wonderful change in the scenery. This pass, though it does not lie across the main watershed between India and Central Asia, like the Mustagh Pass, yet is on the line of what geographers regard as the true Himalayan range—the continuation of the line of the great peaks, including Mount Everest and Kinchinjunga. And it stands in such a position as to form a barrier to the monsoon clouds which beat up against it from the Arabian Sea. Consequently, here on the north side of the Zoji-la, as I had found on the north side of the Rotang Pass in Kulu, very little rain falls and the mountain-sides are bare and barren. All the way from the plains of Turkestan up to the Zoji-la I had been travelling through barren mountains—austere and grand in the extreme through a greater part of the way, but devoid of vegetation, except in tiny patches in a few favoured spots.

Now, of a sudden, on crossing the Zoji-la, all was changed. With inexpressible relief I looked down upon mountain-sides and valley bottoms amply clothed with trees. I did not regret one moment I had spent among the austerer mountains where all was rock and ice and snow. That was an experience that nothing would have made me miss. But we cannot live on rock and ice and snow. For a time they are good and bracing for the soul. But then we want something more satisfying to our human needs. And as I now looked down into Kashmir the mountains had a more human look about them. The sense of awe fell from me. I was again among mountains in which man could live and roam at pleasure; and among mountains whose highest peaks did not seem so utterly beyond man's reach. I was back from mountains on the titanic scale to mountains on the ordinary Alpine scale to which we Europeans have grown accustomed; and back to where plant and tree and man could together thrive and flourish.

A glowing sensation came over me as I pushed rapidly down the pass, first through outlying birches and then into thick pine forest and flowery meadows. Warm human life seemed to come into me once more. Life seemed extraordinarily easy and pleasant. I was in a wholly different atmosphere, and there seemed nothing else to do except enjoy myself.

And certainly no more fitting place for real enjoyment could be imagined. Kashmir in October is as beautiful as any country in the world. And the Sind Valley, which I was now entering, is perhaps the most beautiful valley in Kashmir. I was ending my journey in a perfect paradise. There was never a cloud: always a deep blue sky and a not too powerful sun. And the trees of the forest—the maples, walnuts, sycamore and chestnuts, among the pines—and the mulberries, apricots, pears and apples on the village lands were clothed in their red and golden autumn foliage. Clear, dancing torrents came splashing down the little mountain valleys to join the main Sind stream. Picturesque villages of chalet-like construction were scattered along the valley bottom. Large flocks of sheep and goats were feeding on the mountain slopes. And the villagers, with their harvest safely in, were happy and content.

Under these delightful conditions I reached Srinagar, the capital of Kashmir, on October 30. The long-looked-for but now dreaded moment had arrived when I should have to make my plunge back into civilisation. I was longing to speak to a countryman of my own again. But I should like to have met him by himself and while still in the wilds. To enter all of a sudden the society of a number together—and countrywomen with them—was a paralysing thought. For my appearance was forbidding. I was dressed, except for a European cap, entirely in native clothes—a long Yarkandi robe with a band round my waist, and with long, soft leather native boots. My beard was rough, and my face was almost black from living night and day in the open and being exposed to the glare of the sun off the snow.

Even the Kashmiris mistook me for a Yarkandi. And I dared not appear before my countrymen like this. So I first made my way to a Kashmiri merchant's shop where I could get some rough clothes of at any rate European shape—a coat and waistcoat and knickerbockers, and stockings—and where I could also have my beard shaved, and get a good wash.

Having spent two hours in effecting this change, I rode off into the European quarter. And civilisation had at least some compensations to make up for its forbidding aspect to one returning from the deepest wilds of Nature. For I here received a telegram of congratulations from Lord Roberts (then Sir Frederick Roberts, and Commander-in-Chief in India). To a young subaltern, and from so distinguished a commander, such a telegram was a very exceptional honour. And I could start off now to India feeling I had given satisfaction to the highest military authority.

* * * * *

In those days the cart-road from India had not reached Srinagar, and the first stage I made by boat down the Jhelum River and across the Wular Lake. Nor in those days had the lumbering house-boats, now so much in use, yet appeared. So I made the journey in one of those light, graceful, fast-moving native boats, with a bed rigged up in the stern and matting awnings to make a screen. This boat was paddled by several men, who sang as they paddled. And as we were going down-stream we moved swiftly along. And if I got tired of sitting lazily in a camp armchair, we just turned in to the bank and I got out and walked.

A completer change from the arid Gobi Desert or the icy Mustagh Pass could not well be. I was in a wide level fertile valley in the very plenitude of its autumn splendour, with the umbrageous Oriental planes, the mulberry, pear, and apple trees in every shade of yellow, red, and purple. And this valley was circled round with snowy mountains rising above it much as the Alps rise from the plains of Lombardy. All was bathed in what seemed to be perpetual sunshine, and over the whole hung a gauze-like haze of deepening blues and violets. Then, as towards sunset we reached the open Wular Lake, a great tranquillity seemed to settle down. The smooth waters of the lake lay like glass, without a ruffle. The sun set behind the mountains in a golden glory. Insensibly followed the sweet stillness of the starry night. And again came to me deep, satisfying peace.

* * * * *

Arriving on the morning of November 2 at Baramula, where the Jhelum River leaves the level Kashmir Valley and, descending rapidly, makes further progress by boat impossible, I rode on to Uri in the afternoon, had dinner at seven with Baines, the road engineer, lay down for a little, and then at midnight started off again, on foot, to reach the point where the newly-made cart-road was in working order. Not only was I eager to get back to India, but I wanted to complete my journey in exactly the seven months for which I had asked leave at Peking. I had left Peking on

April 4. I wanted to rejoin my regiment at Rawal Pindi on November 4.

I stumbled about over the mountain track through the night, and by dawn on the 3rd had reached the cart-road. Here I hired an "ekka," a native cart, with one pony, and in it drove three marches to Kohala, the commencement of British territory. Ekkas are not usually considered comfortable vehicles. But their joltings and shakings were nothing to me at that time. All I had to do was to sit on a fairly comfortable seat with my legs dangling over the side and be jogged along steadily nearer home. From Kohala the road was not in working order, so I had to take to a pony again, and late in the afternoon ride another ten miles up a track towards Murree.

From midnight till about seven in the evening I had been going steadily, but I wanted to push on again as soon as I could. So I started—again on foot—at three in the morning and walked through the pine-trees till I reached Murree, my birthplace, as dawn was appearing. And as no one was yet up I lay down by the roadside and slept for a time. Then I entered an hotel and had some breakfast, and tried to look as unconcerned and accustomed to having meals in hotels as I could.

Then came my final stage. I hired a tonga—a low two-wheeled cart, drawn by two ponies, who gallop hard the whole way, and are changed every half-dozen miles or so. Rawal Pindi is forty miles from Murree, and the descent is from 7,000 feet on the very outlying spurs of the Himalaya to 1,300 feet in the plains of India.

November 4 was a crisp autumn morning, and in the same perpetual sunshine I started off on that last stage, the ponies galloping cheerfully down the mountain road and the plains of India gradually opening out before me. Wonderful sensations were mine as I sat at my ease there beside the driver. My great long journey was at an end. What had seemed so fearfully distant as I rode out of the Legation gate at Peking was now there before my eyes. Every obstacle had been overcome. The great desert had been crossed. Turkestan had been traversed from end to end. The Himalaya had been conquered. And now my goal was actually in sight. It was a sweet, delicious moment. And I enjoy it just as much to-day as I did at the time.

* * * * *

I was driven up to the Mess of my regiment, and as no one was in I went on the regimental lines. There I met the post-corporal riding round with the letters, so I asked if he had any letters for me. He asked, "What name, sir?" I said, "Younghusband. Don't you know me?" for the corporal was in my troop. He replied: "I beg your pardon, sir, but you looked so black." I was indeed burnt almost black, and though I had done my best to polish myself up I suppose I was still very rough. So I went to my bungalow, got out my regular clothes, and returned to the Mess.

Here I was warmly greeted by the Colonel, for Lord Roberts, with his usual kind thoughtfulness, had, besides telegraphing to Srinagar to congratulate me personally, also telegraphed to the Colonel to congratulate the regiment on one of its officers having performed such a feat. And a telegram of this kind from the Commander-in-Chief means much. From my fellow-subalterns I got just the kind of welcome subalterns would give to one of their number who had been away for nearly twenty months while they had to do his duty for him.

By dinner-time I was arrayed once more in my scarlet and gold mess jacket and waistcoat, and seated with about twenty other equally brilliantly apparelled gentlemen, all talking hard and loud, and eating course after course at a table covered with silver plate. I had been up at three that morning and at midnight the day before. I felt in a sort of maze. The din of a mess dinner seemed to stun me. I could not struggle against it. And the variety and richness of the food, in comparison with the simple fare I had had for seven months past, almost made me ill. For some weeks after I came back these mess dinners were a perfect nightmare to me—these combined with the lack of exercise—and often after dinner I would have to go for a long walk round the cantonment to work off the effects of noise and overeating combined.

But I had yet to go to Simla to see Colonel Bell and write out a preliminary report of my journey. Colonel Bell had reached India a month previously, and his is therefore the honour of having first travelled from China to India by land. The results of his great journey are recorded in a monumental official report kept secret at the time, and containing most full and detailed information about the populated parts of China and the main trade route across the Himalaya. He was much exercised at having missed me at Hami, the first town I came to in Turkestan at the end of my desert journey. Before he left Peking he had arranged we should meet there on a certain date three months hence. He had arrived exactly on that date and had waited half a day, he said, for me, but then pushed on.

I wrote out my report and have the draft of it now. It is proudly headed: "Report of a Journey from Peking to Kashmir via the Gobi Desert, Kashgaria, and the Mustagh Pass." Then I returned to my regiment. And in the middle of December poor Liu-san, with the ponies, also arrived in Rawal Pindi. He was suffering from pleurisy, caused by exposure in the mountains; but he soon recovered in the warmer air of the plains of India and became his busy, intelligent, cheery self again. He had done me splendid service. He must have been the first Chinaman, for at any rate many hundreds of years, who had travelled from Peking to India. He had served me readily, willingly, and efficiently in every kind of capacity —valet, table servant, cook, groom, transport agent, diplomatist—and he never grumbled. I have no doubt he made money out of me. That I allowed for. But he cannot have made much, for on the whole journey from Peking I spent less than four hundred pounds.

When he was recovered I took him to the railway station. He had never seen a train before, and when the train was drawing up at the platform he exclaimed: "Hai ya! Here's a whole street coming along!" He returned by Calcutta to Tientsin, his native town, and, I heard, rose to affluence afterwards as a kind of courier for European travellers. I hope he is now enjoying a happy old age.

Settling down to regimental life was now for me a true weariness of the spirit. What we had to do was so trivial in comparison with what I had been doing. However, we soon marched off to a camp of exercise and some real soldiering. And Lord Roberts came down to the camp and one night dined with the regiment. We were all assembled at the door of the mess tent, dressed in red mess kit, which we had specially sent for from Rawal Pindi for the occasion, that we might look smarter than in the camp of exercise khaki; and as soon as Lord Roberts had shaken hands with the Colonel he asked for Mr. Younghusband. And his kindness to me then, and his appreciation of my journey, made me feel that I had achieved my ambition, and from henceforth would be regarded as a "traveller"—and this when I was only twenty-four.

I still had many travels in front of me, though, and in the rest of the book I will relate the story of my second journey in the Himalaya—in which the chief obstacle was man rather than the mountains.

CHAPTER VI

RAIDERS AND RUSSIANS

WHAT I had so set my heart on three years before, I had now done. I had seen the great mountains at their grandest, the mightiest peaks, the most fearful precipices and most terrific gorges and the largest glaciers. But I was not yet satisfied. The more you see of the Himalaya the more you want to see. Worse still, as soon as you return you find that far more than you have seen you have missed.

In the summer of 1888 I returned to England for six weeks to give the Royal Geographical Society an account of my journey, for which they awarded me the Gold Medal; but I came back to India feeling positively guilty at the thoughts of my many sins of omission. Geologists had wanted to know if I had observed the rocks; botanists, if I had collected flowers; glaciologists, if I had observed the motions of the glaciers; anthropologists, if I had measured the people's skulls; ethnologists, if I had studied their languages; cartographers, if I had mapped the mountains. To each one it had seemed so easy for me to have made a few simple observations. And to each I must have appeared such a miserably ill-equipped and thoughtless traveller who had simply thrown away his golden opportunities. It would, indeed, have been so easy to observe the rocks, to collect flowers, to measure men's heads, and so on—and so very interesting, too—and I would like to have been able to satisfy these men thirsting so keenly for knowledge. So I returned to India full of good resolutions for the future and deeply repentant of my omissions.

And my next experience of the Himalaya—a few days only after I landed in India on my return—was anything but happy. After three nights and two days in the train in the awful heat of the plains of India in the middle of July, when from the heat and the dust and the noise sleep is almost impossible, I arrived back with my regiment at Rawal Pindi in the early morning, reported myself at the orderly room, and was informed that I should have to ride out to Barakao, thirteen miles, and catch up a detachment proceeding to Murree, and march on foot with them, another thirteen miles, during the night. The immediate prospect was not pleasant; but at any rate I should have a few days in Murree, 7,000 feet above sea-level, where the air would be cool. I caught up the detachment that evening, had a few hours' sleep, and at two o'clock in the morning started to march on foot up the hill to Tret. It is a point of honour in the cavalry that when the men are on foot the officers should be on foot too. But I do not believe that in the whole of my experience I have had a nastier march than that. I was really very tired after my long railway journey, and it was swelteringly hot and the road thick in dust.

I was quite knocked up on arrival at Tret. But Tret is perhaps 3,000 feet high, so much cooler, and I had some amount of sleep there, and the next morning we all set off towards Murree, halting on a spur just below it in a camp which we found ready pitched.

Heavy clouds had been collecting for a day or two past, and the air was sultry and heavy as lead. Towards evening the clouds grew blacker and blacker. About ten, terrific thunder began crashing about us from every side in a continuous roar, and vivid lightning flashed and darted about us without a break. Then a tempestuous wind arose, tearing at the tents and bending the trees. And lastly, sheets of rain came driving down as if they would wash the whole camp off the mountain-side. It was the break of the monsoon, so craved for by unfortunate dwellers in the plains of India, but not welcomed by those in an exposed camp on one of those outlying spurs of the Himalaya which catch it in its full force.

We all, officers and men, had to turn out in the howling wind and drenching rain to make the tents secure. And in the midst of the tumult we were informed by the doctor that one of the men was down with cholera and in a tent which was almost being blown away. Before morning the poor fellow had died. But his was the only case, and we marched on to a less exposed camp beyond Murree. It was cool and pleasant here, and we thought we were free of trouble. But other cases of cholera soon occurred, and one evening I was taken ill myself. Fortunately the doctor's tent was next to mine and he came rushing in as I called to him, and gave me a strong dose of something or other which he said would either kill or cure—nip the cholera before it had time to get way on or be as bad as the cholera itself for me. Probably he was counting on my strong constitution. Anyway, it cured. The tempest inside me subsided almost as suddenly as it had come on. And a week later I was going about all right.

That was my experience of the Himalaya in 1888. Then followed a "cold weather" of drills, and when the leave season of 1889 came on in April I found myself once more pining for the Himalaya. It was tantalising to be so close to the mountains and not to be among them. Often I would ride out from Rawal Pindi to their base and dream of journeys. This regimental life was so arid and meaningless. It was galling to me to feel my youth and keenness and capacity being frittered away. I had hoped the Intelligence Department or the Quartermaster-General's Department would find something for me, but all they had suggested was that I should pass more examinations. I would gladly have entered into the life of a cavalry regiment if the regiment had been really in earnest about training itself for war. But they were not. The Colonel had had me up in orderly room and told me that I was always going on as if we were preparing for active service; but we never went on active service, so it was of no use preparing for it. What we had to do was to prepare to turn out smart for parade when some general came round, and in that way we should get a good name.

Things are very different now. But that was how they were forty years ago. And being so, I was naturally straining to be off where I could be using my superabundant energies and what capacities I had.

Things came to a head when I was on my way to Simla on a few days' leave. In the train was a man keenly interested in my travels; and as luck would have it he asked me when I was going to make another journey. I thought, why not? Why not go to Tibet? That had been my original idea when I was making my trip through Kangra and Kulu five years before: why not carry it out now?

I therefore hatched out a scheme for a journey to Lhasa. I knew the Tibetans would not allow an Englishman to go there. But I might go there in disguise. There flashed across my mind the reflection that when I had arrived in Kashmir on my way from Peking and was dressed in Yarkandi clothes and burnt and rough from the travelling, the Kashmiris had mistaken me for a Yarkandi. Why should I not go to Tibet as a Yarkandi? Why not go up to Leh, get Mohamed Esa and Shukar Ali and go off to Lhasa as a Yarkandi merchant? It was a brilliant idea. And when I arrived in Simla I went straight off to the Foreign Office and asked to see the Foreign Secretary.

Sir Mortimer Durand was most sympathetic. He was amused at my enthusiasm and listened to my plans; but in the end said that it would not do: he could not give me leave. This was a blow, but seeing how sympathetic he was, and feeling instinctively that he was with me all the time, though officially he had to pour cold water, I hastily concocted another scheme for entering Tibet, and this time he laughed and agreed. He said that I was evidently bent on going, so I had better go, and he agreed to give me five thousand rupees for the purpose. This was magnificent. Better than I had ever dreamed of. I hastened back to the regiment and went to the Colonel to ask for leave. But I was met straight away by the most uncompromising refusal. I had been away from the regiment a great deal too much, and it was not fair on the other officers, as my absence prevented their getting leave. This was perfectly true; and I had to admit the point and possess my soul in patience. At a word all my plans had collapsed. And the dry, dull alternative was a hot weather in the plains.

May and June had thus gone by when just at the end of June I received a telegram from the Foreign Office asking me to go on a mission and to come to Simla at once. This was indeed a sudden change in the wheel of fortune. It had come full circle round again, and up went my spirits to apparently the topmost height, though they reached an even higher height when I saw Sir Mortimer Durand and heard from him what he wanted me to do. Readers will remember that on my way to the Mustagh Pass from Yarkand, we passed through country infested by Kanjuti raiders, as they were called in Yarkand—that is, raiders from the remote secluded valley of Hunza, who, issuing from their hidden mountain fastness, were wont to attack the caravans on the trade route from Leh to Yarkand,

and also the inhabitants of the outlying villages of Turkestan as well as nomadic Kirghiz. It was from fear of these raiders that we had to sleep in the open during our passage of the mountains instead of attracting attention by putting up tents. Well, what Sir Mortimer told me was this: On the year following my crossing of the Mustagh Pass, that is in 1888, the Hunza men had raided the caravan route. They had captured a lot of valuable merchandise and held up the merchants to ransom. They had also attacked a Kirghiz encampment near Shahidula and carried off Kirghiz as slaves. The chief, Turdi Kol, had applied to the Chinese authorities for protection, but they had repudiated any responsibility. Turdi Kol had, therefore, applied to Captain Ramsay, the British Commissioner at Leh, for protection, and had undertaken to show us the way to the Shimshal Pass, from whence the raiders issued.

This was one important fact of which Sir Mortimer informed me. The other was more important and more significant. He told me that in the same year a Russian officer, Captain Grombtchevsky, with six Cossacks, had penetrated to Hunza—and Hunza is on the southern, *i.e.* Indian, side of the main watershed, and not on the northern or Central Asian side—had visited the Chief of Hunza and had attempted to form relations with him. Furthermore, the same officer was this year, 1889, contemplating a second visit to this frontier.

Taking these two facts into consideration, the Government of India had decided to send Colonel Algernon Durand to Gilgit to re-establish a political agency there, and from there to visit Hunza and persuade the chief to enter into relations with ourselves; and they had also decided to send me to Shahidula itself, to see Turdi Kol; to get him to show me the way to the Shimshal Pass (about which we knew nothing); to examine this and any other pass of military importance there might be between the Karakoram Pass and the Pamirs; and finally to proceed to Hunza itself and return to India through Gilgit.

Could anything more delightful be imagined? I would be going back to those splendid mountains again, to regions where no white man had ever been; I would be dealing with wild and interesting mountain peoples; I would have every kind of adventure; and I would all the time be doing something of direct and practical value. It was a glorious opportunity, and I meant to use it to the full.

And Sir Mortimer Durand was in every way the man to inspire such an expedition. He meant it to be a success, and he urged me to tell him of whatever I should want to make it a success. I had been selected for the task on account of my explorations in that region in 1887. I must know the conditions better than anyone. And he would like me to tell him what I would require. I was to say if I wanted another officer with me and what escort I required, and what amount of money or what equipment, stores, or instruments. I told him that, as we should have to be many days and even weeks away from any inhabited place and crossing the most difficult mountains, devoid entirely of roads or the roughest paths, my party must be of the smallest and equipped in the simplest way. I would not ask, therefore, for another officer, and would want only sufficient escort to mount guard over my tent at night and a native surveyor to help me with the mapping. And I suggested that the escort should be taken from a Gurkha regiment—preferably the 5th Gurkhas stationed at Abbotabad—as Gurkhas were hillmen and would be best able to stand the hardships of mountaineering.

All the arrangements were approved. The military authorities were asked to arrange for an escort from the 5th Gurkhas and to have them equipped with the warmest clothing and stout boots, and to supply all the necessary camp equipment. The 11th Bengal Lancers were asked to supply a trained surveyor. And I was handed over eight thousand rupees for expenses.

Having completed these arrangements, I returned to Rawal Pindi to get my own kit together and to see about the equipment and stores being supplied by the Commissariat Department, and then I set out for Abbotabad to pick up my escort. On the parade ground the next morning I found the six Gurkhas drawn up, dressed in their new rough mountain kit, and in front of each a pile of the remaining clothes. Each had a good stout poshtin (sheepskin coat), warm jersey, comforter, balaclava (knitted woollen) cap, thick loose coat, and breeches and stout boots, in addition to his ordinary kit, and each was to receive extra rations and extra pay. So each as I finally approved him gave a broad grin of satisfaction and was a source of envy to the whole assembled regiment. And as soon as all were selected I told them to take their kits and get into the ekkas (native carts), which I had ready in the offing, and to drive into Kashmir. I warned them they were going to have plenty of hardships and hard work later on, but that they must drive at first so as to get along as quickly as possible. As they bundled their things into the ekkas and perched themselves up by the drivers they grinned more broadly than ever, and trotted off amidst the wild cheers of their comrades. It was a great send-off. And they deserved it, for they were the sturdiest and stoutest little men in the regiment, and they had plenty to go through before they would be back to their regiment again.

Meanwhile, I had to go round by Murree to pick up my own kit and say good-bye to friends. I had travelled by train and tonga all the previous night, and had still a ride of forty-three miles before me. But it was through most heavenly scenery along that sharp ridge, on an average of about 7,000 feet in height, which forms a kind of outer buttress to the Himalaya, and which on the northward-facing side where the snow lies longest in spring, and which is less exposed to the scorching rays of the sun than the southward-facing slopes, is covered with a thick forest of spruce fir, chestnut, and maple. The road winds along the summit of this ridge, sometimes on one side, sometimes on the other, from the one side giving distant views over the low hills and on to the plains, and from the other side peeps of the snowy ranges of Kashmir, and, from one point, of that glorious mountain, Nanga Parbat, 26,600 feet high.

July 12 I spent at Murree completing my arrangements, and on the 18th finally started on my expedition, catching up my Gurkhas on the following day. They had had a good lazy time of it, driving along in ekkas up the Kashmir road, but the cart-road ended at five marches from Murree, and then I had to put them on ponies. They are splendid little men on foot, but ponies they knew nothing about, and for some days now they spent most of their time in tumbling off. But Gurkhas take everything with a grin, and they seemed to get more enjoyment out of falling off than of stopping on. In this way we were able to do double marches, and avoiding Srinagar we went straight up the Sind Valley to the foot of the Zoji-la Pass, by which I had entered Kashmir at the end of my journey from Peking two years before.

We were now off the hot dusty cart-road and crowded track, and were right up in the cool of the mountains on Sonamarg, the "golden meadow"—so called on account of the profusion of flowers which grow there. Here I found old friends of mine—now Sir Walter and Lady Lawrence—who gave me the warmest of welcomes. And for pure and undiluted joy, brimful and running over, where else could I look than here on this march up the Sind Valley, in a cosy tent, on a flowery meadow, amidst the forests of Kashmir, with trusty comrades round me, with exciting prospects before us, and with old friends in camp close by to whom I could confide the elation I was feeling. These days were the very cream of life. Solitude and company, Nature and man were delightfully intermingled in exactly right proportion. When I wanted solitude I could just walk on ahead or step up the mountain-side by day or close my tent-door of an evening. When I wanted Nature there it was in its manifold and most impressive aspects all round. And when I wanted the comradeship of my fellows the most staunch and faithful of comrades were within hail. Moreover, I was neither shrivelled up by excessive cold, nor enervated by excessive heat, nor soaked by excessive wet. The weather was neither too cold nor too hot, and it was dry and fine. And though hardships and dangers were to come in plenty, the anticipation of them only made me more sensitively appreciative of the present.

But after crossing the Zoji-la, the last pass on my way from Peking, these delights vanished, and we passed through a dreary expanse of bare, brown, rounded mountains till Leh, the capital of Ladak, was reached on July 31. And here the real interest of the expedition began. For here I was entertained by Captain Ramsay, the British representative, and the same who had welcomed me at Srinagar on my arrival from Peking two years before, and it was through him that the communications with the Kirghiz had so far been made. Here also was Musa, the Kirghiz from Shahidula, who had brought in the Kirghiz petition for protection from Hunza raids. So I was now able to make a definite plan of operations and make preparations for our march across the Karakoram Pass to Shahidula, and for our exploration of the

Karakoram range from there to the Pamirs and our subsequent entry into Hunza and return by Gilgit.

It was more particularly about the way to the Shimshal Pass and about the character of that pass that I wanted information from Musa. This was the pass by which the raiders sallied out from Hunza. It must therefore be practicable to a certain extent, but to what extent we did not know, and it was important to find out. There was also a mysterious pass called the Saltoro, about which Colonel Durand wrote to me, suggesting that I should explore it. It was believed to lie between the Karakoram Pass and the Mustagh Pass and be a means of communication between Baltistan and Yarkand. But no one who knew about it could be found, and I would have just to look about for a likely gap.

About the risk of attack from the Hunza raiders I was not particularly anxious. I had my Gurkhas, and Colonel Durand was going to visit Hunza from the Indian side. It was not likely, therefore, that I would be attacked. But about transport and supplies I was extremely anxious. Mine was now a much larger party than I had on my journey across the Mustagh Pass two years before, and from my experience then I knew the mountains would be very difficult for animals and that no supplies whatever would be obtainable after I left Shahidula. I would be travelling in a pathless, uninhabited country for several weeks and have to cross deep, strong-flowing rivers, high passes and rough glaciers. Coolies were out of the question, as each man's food would be as much as he could carry. Ponies would be more useful, but even Yarkandi ponies require a certain amount of food. In the end, it was decided to use camels as well as ponies. Good mountain two-humped camels could be collected at Shahidula, and they could be used in most places except where there were glaciers. And as regards supplies, it was decided to have these brought down from Yarkand territory and sent out in depôts along the main valley of the Yarkand River while I explored the various passes.

A week was spent at Shahidula planning these arrangements, arranging also for the transport of my party across the Khardung, Saser, and Karakoram Passes to Shahidula, and for an escort of seventeen Kashmir sepoys, who were to proceed thus far and remain on the trade route during the open season. Then, on August 8, we left Leh for the second main stage of our journey.

And by now I had had time to take good stock of my party. I had, of course, frequently seen Indian regiments on parade, but I had not till now come into personal touch with men of the Indian Army. My Gurkhas and the Pathan surveyor, Shahzad Mir, were therefore a constant interest to me—and a constant delight. Between the Pathan and the Gurkhas there was as much difference as between a Scotsman and a Tyrolese. The Gurkhas were jovial, happy-go-lucky, good-hearted, sturdy little men, who took very little thought for the morrow as long as they were happy and comfortable to-day. The havildar (sergeant), Surabi Tapa by name, was a short, thick-set man who had seen a lot of hard fighting in the Afghan War of 1879-80 and in frontier campaigns. He knew what the serious side of life was, and was ready to meet it stoutly when it came. In the meanwhile, he meant to make the best of things as he found them and enjoy the things of the moment. The naik (corporal) was a sparer man, happy and cheery, but with a constant passion for a fray with an enemy of some kind. The four sepoys were all jolly, sturdy, hardy men, thoroughly pleased with themselves at being on an expedition of this kind. And all of these were incessantly laughing and chaffing with one another and making over and over again the same old simple jokes, at which they never ceased to laugh immoderately, however often they were made. Contrasted with these was the grave, aloof, Shahzad Mir, taking his surveying work very seriously, and seeing in this expedition an opportunity of making a great name for himself; regarding it as a first step in a brilliant career to end in some high position where he would be covered with medals and decorations.

These were my military companions. But I had also with me now my old friend, Shukar Ali, who had accompanied me from Yarkand over the Mustagh Pass in 1887, and who, on hearing I was coming to Ladak, had immediately volunteered to come with me again. He was a great addition to my party, for he had already been tested in the hardest ordeals. I could trust him through and through—except in any fighting—and I knew he would always be cheery. Formerly he had been a pony man: now I made him cook. Not that I expected any fine cooking from him, but I knew that he would produce something or other under however hard conditions, and this much I could scarcely expect of a cook from India or even Kashmir. I should like also to have had Mohamed Esa. He had, it is true, failed at the Mustagh Pass. Still, he was a splendid leader of a caravan, and very hardy. But he was away from Leh, and in his place I therefore engaged a sharp, energetic little man named Ramzan. He was accustomed to go backwards and forwards to Yarkand, and could speak Turki as well as Hindustani. He was placed in charge of all the transport arrangements, and was also to act as interpreter and general diplomatic agent in dealing with the Kirghiz.

We were, therefore, a trim little party of good, hardy, trustworthy men as we set off from Leh on our venture. As far as Shahidula the way was well known, being the ordinary caravan route to Turkestan. But, well known though it might be, the very first pass, the Khardung, 17,600 feet above sea-level, caused me more distress than the Mustagh Pass itself. Why, it is hard to say—except that the rise to it is very steep. Anyhow, from whatever cause it was, I had acute mountain-sickness. My head ached painfully. I had a sense of nausea. Above all, I felt played out and depressed; and gloomy fears came over me as I thought of all the other still higher passes I should have to cross before my expedition was completed. Poor Surabi Tapa, the Gurkha havildar, was also very bad and had to be helped by a couple of men across the snow-slope on the far side of the pass. But we descended as rapidly as we had climbed, and by the time we had reached the valley of the Shayok River we were all as well and cheerful as ever again, and never afterwards suffered as much from mountain-sickness. It is curious, indeed, how mountain-sickness does attack men. There is no doubt that men do become acclimatised to high altitudes. The human organism adapts itself gradually to the changed conditions. But I suppose there are days when a man is not at his best, and fails to adapt himself and suffers in consequence. Perhaps Surabi Tapa and I were in this lowered state of vitality on the Khardung Pass.

The Shayok is only one branch of the great Indus River, but, fed by the vast glaciers of this region, it is in the summer months a mighty rushing river, and crossing it in a ferry-boat on its swirling surface causes wild excitement. The boat is pushed off into the stream and is immediately carried rapidly down, while the men row with all their might to keep its head straight and propel it bit by bit to the opposite shore, while everyone shouts to encourage the rowers, and the rowers shout to encourage themselves, and the river rises and falls in muddy, foam-flecked waves. As the central current is reached it seems almost certain that the boat will be carried helplessly down the stream to rapid after rapid and death and destruction. But the men increase their efforts in a perfect frenzy till the worst of the current is passed. Stiller waters are eventually reached;

and at length bottom is touched on the far shore —perhaps a mile below the point from opposite which the boat had started—and the men roar with laughter and congratulate themselves on having bested the river.

On the far side we entered the broad, beautiful valley of the Nubra River, covered with apricot-trees and hemmed in by steep, rugged, snow-topped mountains, some of them 23,000 and 24,000 feet in height. And here I met the first caravan of the season to cross the mountains from Yarkand, and I was immediately in the thick of Central Asian politics. The caravan was led by a Badakshi and an Andajani, the first from a province of Afghanistan, and the other from a province of Russian Turkestan. They were both, in a way, cultivated men; that is, they had excellent manners, could express themselves freely and gracefully, and had had considerable experience of peoples of many different nationalities. They were obviously men of enterprise and spirit, for their homes were far distant from where I now met them, and they had ventured across these tremendous mountains, even after a raid had so recently occurred. Neither the perils of high passes, cold, snow, glaciers and torrents, nor the risks of attack by raiders had deterred them. And though the expectation of big profits on the sale of their merchandise may have been one incentive, I can hardly think it was the chief. And I cannot help believing that a love of adventure was a much more potent factor.

With such men it was a pleasure to talk. And

I eagerly picked out of them all they could tell me about the state of affairs at Shahidula where the raid had occurred, and also about the activities of the Russians. From them I gathered that after the raid Turdi Kol, the Kirghiz chief at Shahidula, had first gone to the Chinese to ask for protection, and on the Chinese refusing had come to us. All was now quiet at Shahidula, though the Kirghiz were still very nervous. As to the Russians, these merchants informed me of the presence of a Russian party in Yarkand who were, they thought, making either for Tibet or Leh. And at this information I naturally pricked up my ears, for in those days British and Russians used closely to watch each other's movements in Central Asia. The plot was beginning to thicken, and two days later I heard from a Peshawar merchant just come down from Yarkand that a considerable Russian party had entered the Kuen-lun Mountains and were not very far from Shahidula itself. So I became still more impatient to reach that place without any preventable delay in case I might be forestalled by Russians.

The Saser Pass was not so difficult at this time of year as it often is. But on the day after we crossed it a terrible squall of snow and rain overtook us, and on looking back I saw the pass was hidden in a cloud as black as night; and it is because of these terrific storms that the pass is so much feared. On the far side I found the Kirghiz, Sattiwali, with thirteen camels waiting for me, and I pushed on by double marches ahead of my escort. And it being the regular caravan season, I met several caravans, from all of which I gleaned some bit of information. For these Central Asian merchants are great politicians and keenly enjoyed the rivalry between us and the Russians. One caravan was of Andajanis—Russian subjects. They were a masterful, independent set of men who evidently thought themselves as good as anyone else and better than most. But they were hospitable all the same, as are most of these jolly travelling merchants. And when I strolled over to their camp from my own the head of the caravan politely asked me in to tea and would not take my first excuse, but caught me strongly by the arm and carried me off to his tent, where he produced some excellent tea. Once inside the tent everything was snug and warm and comfortable. A thick felt was spread on the ground, and a little carpet gave colour as well as warmth. My host was most genial and agreeable, and talked much about Turkestan and India. After I had returned to my camp I sent him over a handsome turban of Kashmir shawl material. He immediately put it on and came to my camp to thank me for it, salaaming, and saying it would keep him nice and warm on the cold journey before him.

Dreary marches over the Depsang Plain followed, and on August 19 we crossed the Karakoram Pass. Of all parts of the world this is the most God-forsaken—dreadful in every way. The plain itself is over 17,000 feet above sea-level, and consists of an open expanse of gravel, bounded by rounded, dull, barren hills. Across it incessantly sweep winds of ercing cold. And even now in August heavy snow was falling, there were ten degrees of frost at night, and little streams were frozen hard. To add to the gloom the plain is strewn with the bones of animals who have succumbed to the strain of carrying loads at these great heights. And the Karakoram Pass itself, though it is nearly 19,000 feet in height and across the main watershed of Asia, has nothing impressive about it. It is not even covered with snow. Snow falls, but in small quantity and in powdery flakes, and is soon blown away by the daily tempests.

Pressing rapidly on, I marched thirty-six miles on the following day, crossed the Suget Pass, 17,600 feet in height, and began to descend steeply toward Shahidula. Many caravans were passed, all armed and on the alert, for this was considered the dangerous part of the road. And from these traders I heard rumours that the Russian party was at Kugiar and was believed to be on its way to Lhasa. On August 21, at Suget, I met a man who was to render invaluable aid to me in the weeks to come. He was an inhabitant of Bajaur, an independent state just beyond the Indian frontier, near Peshawar; and he had settled here for six years, making a good business out of selling grain to the passing caravans. He had ridden out to meet me, and was well dressed in the loose many-coloured robes of Turkestan, and riding a good horse with a smart well-turned-out saddle and saddle-cloth. His first appearance did not impress me favourably, for he had a rather cunning look in his small eyes. But he was quick, alert, and resourceful; and I soon found that he meant to be and could be extremely useful—to his own profit, no doubt, but also to the advantage of my expedition, which was the main thing I cared about. He was, in fact, just one other of those adventurous spirits one used to meet in Central Asia who have to live by their wits, endure great hardships, and often suffer heavy losses, but who at times bring off big coups, and in the intervals between big risks and exertions have a lazy, cheery time in some Central Asian town.

Jan Mohamed was the most intelligent man I met in these parts, and he was able to tell me more particulars about the raid of the previous year; for it was on this place, Suget, and not on Shahidula, that the raid had been made. In the beginning of September eighty men had come from Hunza by the Shimshal Pass and up the Yarkand River, crossing my track of the year before—that is, 1887. On arrival at Suget they seized some men out of their tents. One of these was ordered by the Hunza men, on pain of being shot dead, to tell them where Turdi Kol, the chief of the Kirghiz, was. He led the raiders to Turdi Kol's tent, but shouted to him, and Turdi Kol, suspecting something wrong, seized his gun, and as he opened the door of the tent shot a raider on the threshold and the rest fled. Jan Mohamed was not there at the time, but as soon as he returned he set off with Turdi Kol in pursuit of the raiders. They did not, however, catch them up, and the raiders carried off twenty-one Kirghiz and a quantity of merchandise.

On August 28 I reached Shahidula—that is, in less

than two months after I had first been summoned to Simla. From the plains of India I had marched 640 miles through the mountains in just six weeks. So I was well up to time, and could look forward to accomplishing my task before winter set in.

CHAPTER VII

MEETING THE KIRGHIZ

As we approached Shahidula Turdi Kol, the chief of the Shahidula Kirghiz, came riding out to meet me. I daresay he was not more than fifty, but to me in those days fifty was "old," so I put him down as old. He was very careworn in appearance, which is not surprising, as he had already once been captured by the Hunza raiders and had only just escaped being captured a second time. And living a nomadic life as these Kirghiz do, dwelling not in compact defensible villages, but in felt tents peculiarly open to attack, he was naturally in a constant state of anxiety. He was very grave and sedate in demeanour, and very dignified. There was no trace either of arrogant independence or of cringing dependence. He was just respectful and polite—respecting himself and respecting his fellows. He had about him, too, an air of authority, as if he were accustomed to being looked up to. I could see that he was not as quick, alert, and resourceful as Jan Mohamed. But I could see, too, that he was a man of influence and one who could be trusted.

After the first few complimentary speeches he at once started to tell me about the raid last year and of his being awakened from sleep by a man calling to him, and from the very fact that the man called to him from the outside, instead of in the usual way opening the tent-door, being put on his guard, so that he instinctively seized his rifle and shot the raider. He then told me how his people, from fear of these raiders, had had to withdraw from the valley and live on the other side of the Sanju range, nearer the plains of Turkestan. This was a great inconvenience to them and a loss of pasturage for their flocks and of profit on sales to traders on the caravan route.

Having thus eased himself of what was chiefly on his mind he warned me that Sattiwali, the Kirghiz who had first met me, was too impetuous, and that I must be cautious in trusting all he said. Seeing that he was a prudent, careful man, I told him that there was not the least necessity for hurry. At Shahidula I would be halting some days, and he, Turdi Kol, would be close by, and we could discuss the situation at leisure. I had plenty of time, and he could come and talk to me to-day, to-morrow, or whenever he liked. The result of this humouring of him was that he forthwith proceeded to discuss the situation in full, relating all his negotiations with the Chinese for protection, and ending up by saying that if we British did not now help the Kirghiz they would indeed be in a bad way. The poor man was in the extremity of anxiety, and all now depended upon what I was prepared to do.

I quickly relieved his anxiety. Without entering into the question of whether Shahidula was or was not within the limits of the Chinese Empire, I said that Government were taking measures to stop the raids. Colonel Durand was going to Hunza from Gilgit, and I myself intended to go there by the Shimshal Pass. He immediately made me speeches of profuse thanks and declared that if this were done the Shahidula Valley would again become fruitful and the Kirghiz live in peace.

At Shahidula there was the remains of an old fort, but otherwise there were no permanent habitations. And the valley, though affording that rough pasturage upon which the hardy sheep and goats, camels and ponies of the Kirghiz find sustenance, was to the ordinary eye very barren in appearance, and the surrounding mountains of no special grandeur. It was a desolate, unattractive spot. Still, unprepossessing as it was, the Kirghiz did not care to be done out of their right of occupancy by the risk of raids from Hunza robbers.

After I had had a bath, changed, and settled down in my tent I sent word to Turdi Kol that if he cared to continue our talk to-day I was quite ready to see him, or he might come to-morrow if he preferred. He came at once, and we had a long interview. As he was a deliberate old man, I told him to take his time and tell me slowly and clearly all that was in his mind. He began by saying that his father and grandfather had been heads of these Kirghiz, and that in their time all the valley of the Yarkand River, right up to the Taghdumbash Pamir had been inhabited. Even now the remains of a fort which had been built by them at Sarukwat could be seen. But afterwards the Hunza men had raided the country and the Kirghiz had retired to Shahidula. When Yakub Beg was ruler of Turkestan—he was the ruler in Robert Shaw's time—there was a fort at Shahidula, and the trade route was protected. But now the Chinese were rulers of Turkestan they did nothing. Not being able to get any satisfaction from the Chinese, he wished now to transfer his allegiance to the British.

I replied that I had no authority to accept their allegiance and could only refer his request to the Viceroy. But I told him again that we meant to stop the raids, and that he might relieve his mind of that fear. And our business talk being over, and he having agreed to come to the Shimshal Pass with me, I had tea brought, and on his leaving presented him with a handsome robe and turban, both of which he immediately put on and went away salaaming profusely to me, while all his attendants outside the tent salaamed and shouted "Mubárak! Mubárak!" (Good luck! Good luck!)

This conversation I followed up on the next day by a grand Durbar. All the morning I made arrangements, for I wanted it to be an impressive affair. Orientals—and Occidentals too, as far as that goes—love a big ceremony. They also love presents. So I selected and ticketed presents for each of the leading men. And I instructed the havildar and Shahzad Mir exactly what was to be done in minute detail. Then as the time for the holding of the Durbar approached I had a chair and table put on a carpet on an open grassy space. Opposite the chair all the Kirghiz seated themselves. On each side were eight Kashmiri sepoys with fixed bayonets, and behind the chair were the six Gurkhas, also with fixed bayonets. All were in full-dress uniform—not khaki—which I had made them bring especially for such occasions. At the fixed time I myself appeared, proudly arrayed in my scarlet full-dress King's Dragoon Guards uniform. With me was Shahzad Mir, carrying a drawn sword. And as I approached the assembly the Gurkhas fired a salute of three volleys, the Kashmir sepoys presented arms, and all the Kirghiz rose to their feet and salaamed deeply. I then took my seat with Shahzad Mir standing by my side, his sword still drawn, and the Kirghiz again seated themselves on the ground.

Very slowly and deliberately I then repeated what I had already told Turdi Kol. And all the Kirghiz together, taking the time from Turdi Kol, bent forward on their knees, bowing nearly to the ground. Then they rose together and then bowed a second time. It was most impressive out in the open, in that mountain setting, to see these rough nomads bowing there before me. Some strong arm was now protecting them, they felt. Henceforth they could live in peace—and indeed have lived in peace—and their relief was clearly manifest. I then asked them if they had anything to say on their part, and as they wished to say nothing further I proceeded to distribute presents to Turdi Kol and six other headmen who formed a kind of council, each set of presents being taken by Ramzan and placed at the feet of each recipient. To Turdi Kol, Sattiwali, and Jan Mohamed I gave a revolver each, and robes and turbans, and to the others shawls, chintzes, puttoo (Kashmir native cloth), and kerchiefs. Then I called each up separately, and gave to Turdi Kol one hundred rupees, and to each of the others twenty rupees.

After this present-giving I made them another speech. I said they must not look entirely to the British Government for help: they must help themselves. First of all, they must agree to obey their chief. I understood that Turdi Kol was their chief: were they ready to obey him? They shouted they were. I said I would then give him 800 rupees, which was to be spent on repairing the fort so that they could use it as a place of refuge, and I handed him over the money. This closed the proceedings, and as I rose to return to my tent the Gurkhas fired another salute of three volleys.

The result of this meeting was that Turdi Kol came to my tent and expressed himself ready to do anything for me. He gave me all the information he had about the country between Shahidula and the Pamirs, and said he would help me with men, supplies, camels, ponies, anything he could, and would himself come with me to Hunza. This meant a great deal, and did in fact result in the eventual success of the expedition.

The Russian expedition, meanwhile, was moving about in a leisurely way in the mountains between Shahidula and Yarkand. It was led by Colonel Pievtsof, and claimed to have no other than scientific objects.

I had done what I could for the protection of the trade route. I had now to arrange for the second part of my programme—the exploration of any passes there might be leading across the main range. I was on the northern—the Central Asian—side of the Karakoram section of the Himalaya; I had to put myself in the position of a Russian officer looking about for any opening by which he could take a small force on to the Indian side and stir up trouble for us among the peoples who inhabit those regions. More especially had I to explore the Shimshal Pass—by which the Hunza men raid into Turkestan—and the fabled Saltoro Pass leading into Baltistan. I calculated that this would occupy me seventy days till I reached Hunza, and as all the country I would be passing through would be uninhabited, very elaborate arrangements for supplies and transport had to be made. And here it was that the help of Turdi Kol and Jan Mohamed was so valuable. For the actual arrangements Jan Mohamed was the readier and quicker, and undertook to go himself to Yarkand territory to collect the needful supplies. But Turdi Kol's influence was no less valuable. And the fact of his accompanying me himself made all the other Kirghiz willing to come forward.

The crucial moment of the whole expedition would be when we arrived at the Hunza outpost, called Darwaza, on this northern side of the Shimshal. This was the stronghold from which the robbers made their raids. If they chose to stop us there would be the end of the expedition and I should not be able to examine the Shimshal Pass. Turdi Kol had been carried off a prisoner by that way, and I asked him about it. He said the outpost was a fort with a wall on each side of it at the top of a ravine, and that the first man to appear there would certainly be shot. This sounded unpleasant, but I turned to the Gurkha corporal and said in chaff that in that case I would send him first. He grinned with delight and said, "Mind you do, Sahib."

Every arrangement having been made, and the Kashmiri sepoys having been instructed to return to Leh before winter set in, my own little party left Shahidula on September 8, our first objective being the Saltoro Pass.

CHAPTER VIII

SEARCH FOR THE SALTORO PASS

The real excitement of the expedition was now to begin. For some days we should be marching over known country. And then would come the plunge into the unknown. Our first march led up a valley inhabited, till the previous year, by Kirghiz, but now deserted on account of the raid in which several men had been captured. Then we crossed the Sokhbulak Pass into the valley of the Yarkand River. Here the weather was delightful—not too hot and not too cold—and bright and clear. And as we were at comparatively low altitudes, about 18,000 feet above sea-level, we were free from that lowering, depressing feeling we had had in the region of the Karakoram Pass and the Depsang plains. We were able to enjoy life, and with the prospect of adventure now near at hand we marched light-heartedly down the valley; and on September 6, after passing Chiragh-saldi (the place where I had struck the Yarkand River in 1887), we arrived at Urdok-saldi—a refreshing green meadow with plenty of brushwood for fires.

Other good grassy camping-grounds we passed, and I took advantage of its being Sunday to halt at one, both to give the ponies a chance of a good feed before facing the hardest mountains and also to give myself a rest. For on marching-days I had my time occupied pretty well all day long—surveying on the march, seeing the caravan over bad places, collecting information of various kinds from the Kirghiz, and in the evening writing up notes, making sextant observations to the stars for latitude, and initiating manifold arrangements. So a Sunday's rest was always acceptable when I could manage it.

Having had a welcome rest, we headed straight at the Aghil range by the route I had followed two years before. And again I pressed on eagerly to see the view from the summit—the view of the great main range, the passages across which I had now to examine. I remembered well how deeply impressed I had been on my former journey by the sight that then met me. And I was half afraid that this time I should be disappointed. I might have an exaggerated remembrance of its effect upon me and of its grandeur and sublimity, and find that when I saw it again, in cold blood, as it were, I should find it nothing so very much out of the ordinary after all. But I was to suffer no such disappointment. I was, indeed, to be astonished at how much it exceeded my remembrance. The boldness, the ruggedness, the precipitous character of the peaks, and their dazzling brilliance, far surpassed my recollections. And with all my subsequent experience of the Himalaya I do not know of any view quite so impressive of its kind. I have seen views of single peaks more impressive. And I have seen from a considerable distance a more extensive panorama. What was so striking about the view of the Karakoram range from the Aghil Pass was that a phalanx of the very highest peaks in the world—except Mount Everest—could be seen just across the way, and rising with bold abruptness from a valley not more than 12,000 feet above sea-level. I have no doubt, too, that there was some kind of added charm from the thought that only very few men had ever viewed this scene —or ever would. It is one of the inmost sanctuaries of all the Himalaya.

And right into the very midst of these glorious, but most formidable, mountains I was now to plunge. I had already wrested from them one great secret—the secret of the Mustagh Pass. I had to extract two others — the secrets of the Saltoro Pass and of the Shimshal Pass. And first the Saltoro. Away up the valley of the Oprang River I could see a great glacier coming down from the line of the high peaks, and I assumed that it must be somewhere in that region that I should find the pass. From not one of the men I had met could I gather the slightest inkling as to where it was. No one had ever heard of it. It was only from the Indian side that rumours of the existence of such a pass had come. And all those rumours were extremely vague. So I had to grope about entirely in the dark, and with very limited time at my disposal, for I had still to explore the much more important Shimshal Pass, and any passes there might be from the Pamirs into Hunza, and get back through Hunza to Kashmir before winter set in.

We descended from the pass to the valley of the Oprang River and marched up it for a few miles to a spot which I called Durbin Jangal, where there was good grass and plenty of brushwood for fuel. And here I meant to leave the bulk of the party and proceed with a few men to explore the mountains.

Now the crucial work was to begin. All the Gurkhas were to be left behind. But I was to take with me Shahzad Mir to help in the survey; good old Shukar Ali because he had been over the Mustagh Pass with me and I knew he would turn his hand to anything; a Balti to carry a load when the ponies had to be left behind; and one other man to look after the five ponies. I took two small single-fly tents, one for the men and one for myself, 100 pounds of flour, some rice, tea, brandy, ghi (clarified butter), dried apricots, one sheep, and 200 pounds of barley for the ponies. I had also for myself two tins of beef, a tin of condensed milk, a tin of butter, and two jars of Liebig, so that I was very well off in comparison with what I had been on my exploration of the Mustagh Pass. Besides these things we had, of course, our bedding and warm clothes, cooking utensils, and for the survey a sextant and artificial horizon, a prismatic compass and an ordinary compass, a telescope, two watches, two aneroids, and some stationery.

On September 12 we set out marching up the broad valley with the great peaks towering to incredible height above us on our right, and we halted for the night close under the great Gusherbrum peaks, four of which are over 26,000 feet in height. Tremendous giants they were, with fearful precipices on their flanks, and their summits glistening in the purest white against the bluest sky.

Next day our adventures began. An immense glacier came down from the Gusherbrum peaks right across the Oprang Valley, and would have impinged upon the stupendous cliffs of the far side if the river had not just managed to keep a way for itself between the cliffs and the end of the glacier. The glacier at its end was nearly two miles broad, and the central portion was a conglomeration of dazzling icy sèracs. The view up it, with the Gusherbrum peaks at the head, was one of the great sights of even this region. But for the moment I could not let my mind dwell upon its grandeur, for all my energies had to be devoted to getting the ponies along, squeezing them in, as it were, between the glacier and the cliff. No other ponies than these wonderful Yarkand ponies could have done it. And no one else than Shukar Ali would have dreamed of attempting it. For great blocks of ice were continually being washed off the end of the glacier, and the river had to be crossed four times when neither on the cliff nor on the glacier the most precarious foothold could be found.

Eventually this obstacle was negotiated, and then we found ourselves in a wide part of the Oprang Valley, and had to make up our mind as to which of three branches into which it divided we should ascend. The main valley led up in a south-south-east direction towards the Karakoram Pass, in the neighbourhood of which the Oprang apparently took its rise. But a tributary valley to the right seemed to me to lead in the direction of where it was believed the Saltoro Pass must be; so I chose that.

This valley was completely filled with a glacier, which I named the Urdok glacier because I saw a duck on it, and "urdok" is the Turki for a duck. And as the mountain-sides on either hand were precipitous, we had to bring the ponies up the moraine of the glacier. I used to pioneer on ahead for a way, while Shahzad Mir surveyed, and Shukar Ali and the two men brought the ponies along. Shukar Ali was as splendid as ever, but I pined for my other Mustagh men—Mohamed Esa, Wali, and Turgan.

The glacier was bad enough on the first day. On the second it was worse. I climbed the mountain-side to a height of nearly 2,000 feet, hoping to get a view ahead, but snow-clouds kept hiding the mountains. And most curious snow-clouds these were. Almost imperceptibly a sharp, well-defined peak would become more and more obscured, till eventually it faded from view altogether. A cloud of the finest snow had gradually formed itself and enveloped the mountain. Rejoining my party from the climb, I at first found a fairly easy way, and we got along comfortably enough. But soon we were brought up by a terrible jumble of blocks of ice, white on the surface but showing a beautiful transparent green wherever broken. I formed a plan of carrying the loads over the ice and swimming the ponies across a glacier lake. But on exploring further I found it worse still ahead. So we had to retrace our steps and attempt some other way up the glacier. Having done this we were, however, again brought to a halt by some crevasses, and there we had to halt for the night—I, at least, thoroughly tired out.

Next day, September 15, we retraced our steps for a second time, and now at last we did find a way up the glacier and by the afternoon reached the comparatively smooth ice at its head and encamped close under a gap in the range, which I presumed must be the Saltoro Pass. But, if so, it looked no better than the Mustagh Pass. It was nothing but a wall of ice and snow for well over 1,000 feet—passable, no doubt, for expert and properly equipped mountaineers, but no pass in the ordinary acceptance of the term.

That night Shukar Ali and I took counsel together as to our mode of attack. We had reconnoitred ahead in the afternoon, and we determined to make a start the next day well before dawn, and try to reach the top of the pass by midday, and so have time to get back to our camp before dark. At 2 a.m. on the 16th we were astir, but did not actually get off till 3.30. There was a hard frost. It was snowing hard. And there was so little light from the moon behind the clouds that we could scarcely grope our way along among the crevasses. No true mountaineer would have dreamed of attempting the pass on a day like this, and I was foolish to have proceeded. But I could not afford the time to wait for the snow to stop falling and consolidate, and in ignorance of the danger I was incurring I went on.

As we ascended higher the crevasses became less frequent, but the going continued heavy, for we were trudging through fresh deep snow, sinking up to our knees at each step. Day dawned, but the snow-fall did not cease. The upper parts of the mountains were hidden in the clouds and we could not see the pass. We knew its general direction, though, and soon began to ascend an ice-slope towards it. We roped ourselves and cut steps in the ice, and were proceeding steadily upward when suddenly out of the snow-cloud in which we were enveloped we heard above us a fearful, tearing, rushing roar approaching us nearer and nearer. We could see nothing on account of the cloud. But we knew at once it was an avalanche, and it seemed to be coming straight down on the top of us. Our first instinct was to run. But we could not run, for we were on an ice-slope, so we crouched in an agony of fear. And just as it seemed to be crashing right upon the top of us the avalanche rushed past us just ahead in the very ravine we were about to enter. If the avalanche had started a few minutes later or we had advanced a hundred yards farther, we would have been swept away and no one would ever have known what had become of us.

Still blind to the risks I was running and undeterred by the danger we had so narrowly escaped, I pressed on through the snow-clouds, up the icy slope, to a point where a great yawning chasm in the ice made further advance impossible—unless, indeed, we had ventured into the ravine down which the avalanche had shot, and down which another might shoot at any moment; and to do that even I was not sufficiently foolish.

So we turned back and gave up all hopes of reaching the supposed Saltoro Pass. I had seen quite enough to make sure that there was no practicable way by which a military force could cross the range in this direction; and that, after all, was the main object of my efforts, for I was not out on a mountaineering expedition pure and simple. And, as Dr. and Mrs. Bullock-Workman many years afterwards found, even if I had reached the gap I was making for, I should only have entered another vast glacier region—the Sia Chen glacier—and there would still have been another pass to cross before the Saltoro Valley in Baltistan was reached.

We hurried back, then, down the ice-slope, only anxious to be off it and out of danger from the avalanches as quickly as possible. On our way we saw another avalanche come rushing down the mountain-side and cover up the actual footsteps we had made on our ascent. So twice had we escaped destruction; and very thankful I was when we were out on the open glacier and free from all danger—anyhow, of avalanches, though we still had to beware of crevasses.

* * * *

On occasions like this a man feels brought straight up against Nature in her most terrible form; and I find recorded in my diary the following observations made, as a matter of fact, in our glacier camp *before* our experience of the avalanches: "We have to trust to someone higher than man to lead us through everything safely. The mere slip of the foot might often send us to destruction, and even very trifling mishaps might spoil the success of the undertaking. So that we cannot but feel that any success that may come in the end is due to an overruling Providence and not to our own feeble efforts."

But on reading this over thirty-four years after it was written, and in the light of further experience and deeper thought, I doubt whether it accurately expresses the true state of affairs or represents the attitude of mind a man ought to have in the presence of the stern forces of physical Nature. I evidently had in my mind the idea that these physical forces were the enemy, as it were, and that I was specially watched over and guarded by some invisible Being, quite outside and apart from myself, who in some unseen manner guided my footsteps so that I did not fall, and would divert the course of an avalanche so that it would not crash upon me. It was the attitude of mind in which I was brought up, and I accepted it without thinking out its implications.

But when I consider how that splendid mountaineer, Mummery, was swept away in an avalanche on Nanga Parbat in Kashmir, three or four years later; and when I think how often in my experience poor coolies carrying the post across the Kashmir mountains have been carried away in avalanches, it now seems to me simply shocking that I should have had the presumption and conceit to think that I was specially marked out for favour while these poor men were left to destruction. If anyone deserved destruction it was myself, for not properly using the judgment with which I had been endowed.

The physical forces of Nature operate according to certain laws. And we have to know those laws, for it is because we can absolutely rely upon their unbroken constancy that we can work with them and through them, and so accomplish our own human ends. I was perfectly right in trusting God. But my conception of God was a poor and meagre one. And my conception of myself in comparison with the brute forces of physical Nature was no less meagre. In neither case did I realise that God was within me as well as above and around me; that I was a part of God; and that these physical forces were controlled by God. I did not realise my greatness in face of the physical forces, and I did not realise my responsibility for using my faculties to the utmost. The physical forces arrayed against me—though only apparently against me—were tremendous. Cold and snow and ice and wind. But by taking thought, by profiting from experience, and by co-operation, man can conquer these forces. Man can clothe himself against the cold, he can study snow conditions and bide his time till they are safe, and he can equip himself to minimise the risks and hardships. There is no need, then, for him unduly to depress himself by his insignificance in comparison. And when he looks within himself, and still more when he looks within that great Whole, of which he and his fellows, and the animals and plants, and great mountains and the stars above them, all form part, he will find a far greater God sustaining, maintaining, and directing it than ever I had pictured that Providence directing my footsteps on the mountain. A Providence was indeed directing me: but He was directing far more than my footsteps. He was directing my whole being, and directing it to higher things. This Providence was expecting of me that I should use the *whole* of myself—my judgment as well as my will and affections—that I should exercise wisdom as well as practise goodness. And if trust be placed in such a God, as the source of all goodness, wisdom, and beauty, then strength will accrue to us. We shall be able of ourselves to plant our own footsteps aright and confront with confidence physical Nature in her sternest aspects and come to love her even in her austerest moods.

* * * * *

On arrival back in our camp we acked up and marched on down the glacier thou h it was still snowing hard. Through the night continued to snow heavily, and the next mornin tents, ponies, baggage, all were covered with thick snow, and again through a snowstorm we marched on down the glacier till in the afternoon we reached a spot at the end of it where there was a certain amount of grass for the ponies and scrub for fuel, and where there was sand to lie on at night instead of the hard, sharp moraine of the glacier with the ice just below. Snow still fell heavily during the night, but the next day, September 18, I got back to my main camp at Durbin Jangal, where my Gurkhas were. And to receive their cheery welcome, and then turn into my full-sized "Kabul" tent, in which I could stand upright, and where there was a bed, and a table and a chair and a bath, was like getting back to the very acme of civilisation. And then, after a bath and a change into clean clothes, and a good dinner, to settle down in a comfortable chair with a book and be transported away from every hardship into the heavenly region of the spirit, was one of the supremely good things life has to give. So Durbin Jangal, where I halted for a couple of days and where I took many sextant observations to the stars and to a tremendous peak which rose sovereign over all the rest, and which I mistakenly took for the peak K_2, is one of the spots in all the world I remember with the greatest pleasure.

CHAPTER IX

REST AND REFLECTION

FROM the strain of travel one wants some relaxation. I had therefore brought with me just a few books. They were an odd variety: Monier Williams' "Buddhism," Lubbock's "Ancient Civilisation," "The Childhood of the World," "The Childhood of Religions," "Nicholas Nickleby," and "The Old Curiosity Shop," various official reports, the Royal Geographical Society's "Hints to Travellers," Momerie's Sermons, a Bible and Prayer-Book. In these I now revelled. I was now twenty-six years of age, and I was strung up to the highest pitch of being. Though far remote, at the very back of the Himalaya, I could feel the expectation of Government strong on me to conduct myself worthily. I had a splendid lot of men about me who were as dependent on my skill and nerve for their lives as I was upon their fidelity and endurance for mine. Neither Nature nor man would allow us to be at anything else but our best. And in this time of most strenuous action I had these two days of profoundest meditation, and they crucially affected my whole outlook on life.

I had by now been seven years with a regiment; I had seen a good deal of India; I had travelled right across the Chinese Empire from the extreme east to the extreme west; I had lived under the closest conditions with a great variety of men; I had travelled through great forests in Manchuria; I had traversed the greatest desert in the world and crossed the highest mountains; and in the desert and the mountains I had spent many a night in near communion with the stars. Naturally, therefore, I was inquisitive to know what this wonderful world of which I had seen so much was really like, what was at the bottom of all I saw, what was the central Power which actuated it; and how we really stood in regard to the world, and were connected with it.

When I first started travelling it was the outward aspect of the world that interested me. Now it was the inner character and motive. I wanted to discover the deepest springs of life, to get behind the outward appearance and find the reality which underlies it, as we try to find the real man behind his surface looks. By necessity I had had to be searching for the real thing in men of an extraordinary variety of types. Now I wanted to be searching for reality in the world as a whole. And while I wanted to know all this about the world and our relation to it, I also wanted to know what the world was making for. Then it was only thirty years after the publication of Darwin's "Origin of Species." Evolution was in the air. I was accustomed to looking up to the great peaks about me. What I wanted to know was the highest peak of development man had yet reached, and at what higher peaks he should aim.

Such were the fundamental questions which kept stirring in my mind. It would have been strange if they did not. In our youth we all take our religion — our root attitude to the world — at second-hand and on trust. But a time comes when we feel the need of thinking things out for ourselves and making our own religion. Only by so doing can we feel that religion is any real power in our lives. Especially do we feel this need when we are thrown with men of different religions from our own.

I had had to live with and have my life dependent on men of all the chief religions—Hindus, Buddhists, Confucianists, Mohamedans. Theoretically, the religion of each was very different from the other and from my own. But some great strain or crisis which exposed their souls would show that one and all acknowledged the working in the world of some great invisible Power which in the main was good and certainly expected good of them and not bad. Each naturally thought his own religion was the best. And I was interested to find in what way each differed from the other and in what way our own was the best. I saw, too, that our own was changing—at any rate in externals—under the impact of this new idea, or old idea revived, of evolution; and I had to satisfy myself as to what we had to cling on to with might and main, through thick and thin, and what might be rejected as unessential.

Thus I found myself reaching out with my whole being to get beneath the mere external accessories of my own religion, and of all religion, to the inner essential core and spring—the very motor-centre. I wanted to conserve whatever was good in what I had, like every other young man, received at second-hand; and I wanted to create for myself what would be better than I already had. And this religion which I would make for myself I wanted to test against the strength of the mighty mountains round me, against the lofty purity of their snowy summits, against the piercing radiance of the stars, and against the devoted loyalty of the sturdy men I had about me.

These men all wanted to be good, knew they ought to be good, felt something within them propelling them to be good, and something without expecting them to be good. And in readiness to sacrifice their lives for the good of the expedition they *were* good. The religion I must find must be so transparently clear that any one of these would see that what I prayed to was what they prayed to, what I worshipped was what they worshipped.

✓ So the exploration upon which I set out from Durbin Jangal, and upon which I have been engaged ever since, is the exploration of the very heart and soul of things, the discovery of the real Power, the inner Being, of which the outward features of Mother Earth's face, the plants and animals and we men, are but the expression. This search for the inmost secrets of the world which are the supreme interest for men was the spiritual adventure upon which I then embarked.

And as I set forth I felt that same elation, only to an intenser degree, that I had felt when starting on my first venture into the Himalaya. But I will not describe my experiences here, for they have already been related in my other books.

CHAPTER X

THE RAIDERS' STRONGHOLD

After these two days of refreshing rest and deep spiritual enjoyment I set out with my whole party on my second quest—the secret of the Shimshal Pass. Turdi Kol guaranteed to show me exactly where it was, and of necessity it must have been somewhere to the westward of the Mustagh Pass, for it led into Hunza. But to make quite sure that there was no other pass between it and the Shimshal, I determined to go up towards the Mustagh Pass and then explore the Karakoram range west of it. So I had a last look at that bold, upstanding peak which we could see from Durbin Jangal dominating all the others, and then set off down the Oprang Valley, marching twenty-three miles to Suget Jangal on the tributary which comes down from the Mustagh Pass.

From there, on September 23, I set out with some of the Gurkhas to explore a great glacier region to the westward. Again heavy snow fell, and we had a cheerless time on the rough moraine, amidst the crevasses and séracs of the glacier, with only occasional glimpses of the great peaks of the main range. However, nothing damped the spirits of the Gurkhas. These conditions only seemed to brighten them up, and a joke about looking for some soft stones to lie on kept them in roars of laughter every evening. It had originated in some officer in the Afghan War. But the Gurkhas never tired of it, and the havildar would repeat it with the same success every evening.

We had the greatest difficulty in finding our way through the crevasses, and once we were in the middle of the glacier it was almost impossible to get back on to the mountain-side. Being completely blocked at one point by an intricate series of crevasses caused by a bend in the glacier, I managed to cross a frozen glacier lake on to the mountain-side, and found a promising way along it towards a gap in the range which might possibly be a pass. But when Shahzad Mir tried to follow me he went through up to his waist and only saved himself from drowning by clinging to a big block of ice. Coming back I, too, went through twice and got horribly wet. Still, I thought that by the following morning the ice would bear us, so we encamped close to the lake, and I meant to go on with three men, very lightly laden, to try and reach the gap.

This was September 26, and we had a poor time that night, for we had only a very small amount of firewood—just enough to cook by and not enough to dry our wet boots and clothes by. The thermometer was down to 6 degrees, and we had only snow to lie on. Next morning was, however, fine and sunny, and Shukar Ali, Ramzan, a Balti, and I started out for the gap, while the rest of the party returned to the main camp at Suget Jangal. I had meant to carry a load myself, but when I began to put it on Shukar Ali seized it and would not hear of my carrying one. We found our way down to the lake without difficulty. But there we were brought to a standstill. For the water under the surface ice had drained away and the ice by itself was not strong enough to bear us. I ventured on to it for a few yards, but it kept falling through with sharp reports, so I hurried back. I gave up all idea of reaching the head of the glacier. Evidently, as Turdi Kol had assured me, there was no reasonably practical route into Hunza this way.

Snow fell again in the afternoon, and our sixth night on the glacier was as miserable as the rest. But September 28 was a glorious day of brilliant sunshine. After the heavy snow-fall everything was of purest white, glistening in the sunshine. Away to the south, not twenty miles distant, was the marvellous array of main-range peaks. And over all, clear though it was, there yet lay that finest haze of faintest blue which gives a tender touch to the extreme austerity and wins our heart in spite of all. And there comes, too, in situations such as this, a curious sense of being in a purer world raised far above the turbid life of ordinary humanity. It is a stern world, it is true. And its beauty is of the severest. But it comes as a satisfaction to know that there is such a world as this. It seems to purify our entire being and leave its impress for ever on us. We may not always after remain worthy of it. Still, we have glimpsed its beauty. And the *desire* to be worthy of it can never leave us.

Full of spirits I hurried on ahead of my men to Suget Jangal camp. Seeing me alone the men there hurried out to meet me, thinking some misfortune had occurred to the party. I told them the worst that had happened was that I had got soaked through in constantly wading the river, and wanted a change of clothes and a good dinner. I turned into my comfortable tent as quick as I could, and after having satisfied every creature want to the full, I set to and revelled in my books and had another of those splendidly stirring times of spiritual communion.

We halted a day and then set off for the Oprang Valley, down which we marched for several days. Beyond terrific winds the chief excitement, as we reached lower down and the amount of water increased, was the continually crossing and recrossing of the river. I had the only pony without a load, so upon me devolved the task of finding fords. But even when I had found a fairly favourable spot for crossing, the ponies, instead of making straight across, would let themselves drift away with the current into deep places, and all the baggage would get horribly wet. Everyone would shout and yell and throw stones at the ponies to keep them straight. But with a perversity almost human they made steadily for the deepest pools.

On October 2 we passed the Shimshal River, up which lay the route to the raiders' stronghold and the Shimshal; but as we were running short of grain for the ponies, I determined to march on down the Oprang River to Chong Jangal, where it joins the Yarkand River, for there I expected to meet Turdi Kol with a fresh lot of supplies. I was groping in the dark, for there was no map of this country; it was entirely unexplored. But we presumed the Oprang River *did* join the Yarkand, and hoped for the best.

Alas! just as by my calculations, from observations for latitude to the stars, the Oprang River ought to have struck the Yarkand River, it suddenly turned round and came almost straight back. And this was serious, for the water was getting deeper and deeper. Once or twice I was nearly carried away. And at the end of the day the Gurkhas, who instead of crossing and recrossing had scrambled along the mountain-side, were on the wrong side of the river. I was cogitating how to get them over, when to my horror they proceeded to plunge straight into the river. The water was up to their armpits, flowing strong and icy cold; the bottom was rough; and I was in agony that they would be carried away. However, they stuck bravely to it and emerged soaked through, but with broad grins on their faces, as if it were the greatest possible fun.

Chong Jangal we at last reached on the afternoon of October 4. But there was no Turdi Kol, no supplies, and no post. There was, though, plenty of good grass and plenty of brushwood for fuel, some of the bushes being from fifteen to twenty feet in height. We were, therefore, in luxury. But day after day passed and there was still no sign of Turdi Kol and supplies. And I was beginning to fear we might be stranded in the middle of the mountains with nothing to eat when, to my immense relief, on October 10 he at last appeared with a full supply of all we wanted.

We were now in a position to proceed to Darwaza, the stronghold of the Hunza raiders, on the north side of the Shimshal Pass. We accordingly retraced our way up the Oprang River to the point where the Shimshal River joins it. And this latter we then ascended on October 14 towards the pass. I had received at Chong Jangal an urgent letter from Government, saying that Colonel Durand had been unfavourably received at Hunza, and that therefore I must be careful about entering the country. So I had to proceed on the assumption that I should meet with a hostile reception.

The valley was of the wildest and most rugged description. It was very narrow. The river ran at the bottom of a gorge, and rocky, precipitous mountains, culminating in lofty, snowy peaks, rose on either side. And it was about the remotest valley in the whole Himalaya, for we ourselves had been travelling for forty-one days without seeing a single human being outside our own party. A fitter place for a robbers' den could not be imagined.

We were now approaching the climax of our expedition. And though it might have eventuated in disastrous failure, I had then such buoyancy of youth that the idea never once entered my mind that it would be anything else but complete success. Turdi Kol, Sattiwali, and a few other Kirghiz with camels were with me, and they were by no means so confident. But the Gurkhas were in high spirits at the prospect of meeting these Hunza raiders, and we marched cheerily along, ahead of the baggage, by a rough path which had been worn by the raiders along the mountain-side.

On topping a rise we saw ahead of us a wall with a tower at each end lining the head of a cliff. The cliff formed the side of a ravine running down to the river. And the fort was the raiders' stronghold. It was what is known as Darwaza, or the Gate to Hunza. And it completely blocked the only way into the country. We thrilled with excitement as we at last saw the raiders' lair. And that it was occupied we assumed from the fact that smoke was rising from the tower. The critical moment had indeed arrived. And the question was how now to proceed. I did not want to alarm the Hunza men by suddenly appearing before them with the whole of my party. I thought there would be a better chance of success if I went on ahead with two or three men and parleyed with them, leaving the bulk of the party —a "bulk" which only amounted to six Gurkhas! —to cover my retreat in the event of a hostile reception.

So, taking with me Ramzan to speak Turki and Shahzad Mir to speak Persian, I descended into the ravine, crossed the frozen stream at the bottom, and was proceeding towards the fort when I was joined by the Gurkha corporal, who had run breathlessly after me, saying that at Shahidula I had promised that he should be allowed to go first —this was after the Kirghiz had said that the first to appear at the fort would certainly be killed.

We four, then, climbed the zigzag track up the precipitous side of the ravine towards the wall and towers which lined the top. The door was open, and I thought we should have a peaceable entry, when suddenly the door was slammed, the whole wall was lined with the wildest-looking men, shouting loudly and pointing their matchlocks at us from only fifty feet above us, and in a twinkling it looked as if the worst was going to happen. But fortunately they did not fire, and contented themselves with shouting. So I halted, and we shouted back at them: "Bi adam! Bi adam!"—the Turki for "one man"—and kept holding up one finger and beckoning to them to send one man to parley with us.

At length the clamour ceased, the door of the fort opened, and two men came down to us. I said that I was on my way to Hunza to see their chief, and that Colonel Durand had informed him that I was coming. They said they were aware of this, and an official was stationed three marches distant across the Shimshal Pass to look after me. But the chief had given no orders that I should be allowed to pass, and I must stay where I was till they could communicate with the official. I told them that my supplies were running short and I would prefer to go on. Still, if they had received no orders from their chief to let me pass, naturally I must stay where I was. It does not do to appear to be in a hurry on these occasions. We must assume an air of perfect indifference. The result was completely satisfactory. The men I had been talking to took back my reply to the headman in the fort, who immediately sent back instructions to let me through. I was first, however, to say how many men I had with me, and when the Hunza men had gone to verify my statement and found it true, we were all allowed to proceed.

But at the very last moment an incident occurred which might have ended disastrously. Just as I was riding through the gate between two rows of these wild Hunza men, one of them suddenly stepped out of the ranks and seized my bridle. It looked as though there was treachery, and my Gurkhas were on the point of firing, when the man burst out laughing, and I laughed too. He explained that he only intended it as a joke to try and frighten me. But he was within an ace of carrying a joke that one little bit too far which would have meant death to him and some others besides.

Once we were inside, however, we soon made friends. It was bitterly cold, and the Hunza men lit a huge fire in the open space on the far side of the wall, and round this we all gathered and talked over the situation. I had got the hint from the Kirghiz that the men who actually carried out the raids thoroughly hated the business. They had all the risks and danger, while the chief kept all the profit to himself. They raided because they were ordered to raid, and would have been killed by the chief if they refused. I kept this in mind when talking to these raiders. I explained to them that the Queen of England was naturally very angry at her subjects being raided, and had sent me to see their chief and come to some arrangement with him by which they could be stopped. They said that they could not discuss that with me. And I replied that of course I understood that, but, all the same, I thought they might like to know what I was coming to their country for. It was obvious that they did like to know. And when the little Gurkhas produced some tobacco, and with their customary grin offered it to them, they were completely won.

Only one hitch occurred. They said that everyone with me must go on to Hunza. But I could not take the Kirghiz there. I had hired camels from them up to this point, and they had to take these camels back. The Hunza men insisted the Kirghiz must go on. But now, being on the right side of the wall with my Gurkhas around me, I could take up a different tone, and I told them straight that I was not to be dictated to whom I should take and whom I should leave. If their chief was going to take up that line, then I would go back to India at once and tell the Queen that the Hunza chief was unfriendly. This had an instant effect, and they at once gave in and let the Kirghiz go.

So now I had to part with Turdi Kol, the Kirghiz chief. He had, indeed, served me well. With great pluck he had shown me the way right up to this stronghold. He had also arranged for all the camels, ponies, and supplies I wanted. The Kirghiz of these parts are, on the whole, not a very prepossessing lot. They are hardy, but have little grit. But Turdi Kol was a great exception. He had plenty of pluck, and he had that indefinable quality which comes from good breeding all the world over. He unconsciously commanded respect. And I also regarded him with real affection in addition.

Thus it was that this eventful day passed. And as we sat there making arrangements, with the mountain towering high above us, I thought to myself how wonderful it all was. Here was I, a solitary Englishman, come thousands of miles from my homeland, and now, in the very heart of the highest mountains in the world, laying down the law to a gathering of men extraordinary in their variety—hard, wild, Hunza raiders; softer-spirited but no less hardy Kirghiz; cheerful, pugnacious little Gurkhas; a stern, intelligent Pathan; mild, willing, hardy Ladakhis and long-suffering Baltis—and they were all gladly doing my will.

Often in the thirty odd years that have passed since then have I thought of that position. I am not so insincere as to pretend that my ability to control these different peoples in that remote spot was not due in some degree to myself. Of course it was. And I should have been a poor kind of creature if I had *not* been able to handle such a situation. For the work I was engaged on was that for which I had especially fitted myself; and if I were not reasonably competent on my own particular line there would have been very little use in me. But that I was able to do what I did was *mainly* due to the fact that I was an Englishman, that I stood for the British Empire, and I had at my disposal not only the authority but the good name which England during long centuries had established. For generations Englishmen had been building up an influence and a prestige, and all of this was now at my disposal. So, when I spoke or acted, what these generations of Englishmen—my own father included—had done was expressing itself through me.

For that occasion and to those people I was the representative of England. I was to them the embodiment, the incarnation of the spirit which animates England. I was unconsciously making manifest to those people the spirit of England. I was revealing England to them. And I could feel England expecting me to bear myself in a manner worthy of her. I knew she would reward me if I did well. I knew she would censure me if I did ill. And I knew, too, that all these men, and especially the Hunza men, who had never seen an Englishman before, were eyeing me minutely and through a thousand little ways were forming their opinion of England. Not only from my words, but from my bearing, my manner, my expression, my voice, my way with the Gurkhas, from every little act, they were, like children with strangers, drinking in impressions, and forming their ideas of the character of England.

And when we are in such a position as I was then we realise that our country is a very real *being*. It is in no figurative sense that we talk of England in personal terms as *she* doing this and *she* making that decision and speak of *her* being angry or friendly. In a very real sense she does think and act and feel. She has intelligence and will and feeling, and a quite definite character of her own. She is a real being, as anyone who has represented her in a far-off country very soon knows. He knows he has to act in accordance with her will and intention. If I had thought it was the will and intention of England, and in accordance with her character, I could have taken up a domineering attitude towards the Hunza men, fired upon them, tried to strike awe into them, impressed them with the sheer *might* of England. But I knew very well that that was not her will or in accordance with her character. I knew her intention was that I should by every means possible get on good terms with them, melt away opposition, and induce them to stop raiding and behave in a neighbourly, friendly way toward us. I had no definite instructions to this effect. Definite instructions were unnecessary. I acted as I did because I knew that it was the will of England. There was no mistaking the fact that England had a will. England was quite distinctly a real being with a very real will.

Now, carrying the idea a step further, suppose I could be transported to one of those stars to which I used to take sextant observations for latitude nearly every night. I would appear among the inhabitants of that star as the representative not only of my motherland, but of Mother Earth; and I should feel Mother Earth expecting me to comport myself in a manner worthy of her. I should feel Mother Earth as a whole, and as a real being with a will and intelligence and character, just as at the Hunza post I felt my motherland was.

And carrying the notion still further and regarding the world as a whole—the whole universe—is not that also a real *being* with a will and intelligence and feeling? Can we not feel the world as a whole expecting us to behave in a certain way—expecting us to do the good thing and not the bad, to make the best of ourselves and not the worst, to make ourselves and everything about us beautiful and not ugly, to discriminate truth from error and pursue the truth and not the error. We can all feel that readily enough. And that much alone—and there is a great deal more besides—is sufficient ground for holding that the world is a being with intelligence, will, and character, and a being who may be regarded as Mother World.

These reflections belong, however, to after years. At the moment, I was intent on my next step forward, which was the exploration of the Shimshal Pass. This Hunza outpost, Darwaza, was on the Central Asian, not the Indian side of the main range. I had still, therefore, to cross the range by this Shimshal Pass, which had so far not been explored by a European. Whether it was an easy pass like the Karakoram, or a pass like the Mustagh—fit only for acrobats—we did not know. Nor did we know its exact position. And this was the secret I had now to discover.

After passing through the fort we marched on a mile or two and encamped on a spot where there was plenty of brushwood and we could have a good fire. Seven Hunza men came with us. They were very hardy, determined-looking men, but with not the slightest animus against us, and quite inclined to be friendly. Grain is very scarce with them, and they are accustomed to live on very scanty fare. So when I gave them flour, mutton, tea, and sugar they became more friendly than ever. The next day, October 15, the secret of the pass was at last disclosed. But the Shimshal kept its secret to the very last moment. We still kept up the valley for a mile or two. Ahead of us was the rugged line of peaks of the main range, and in them a gap at a height of about 17,000 feet which I assumed was the pass. But quite unexpectedly we turned off sharp to the right, and there suddenly was revealed a much deeper, broader gap, which proved to be only 15,300 feet above sea-level. After being accustomed to passes 17,000, 18,000, and 19,000 feet, this was indeed a welcome surprise. There was no difficulty in ascending to the pass, and the pass itself was an almost level "Pamir," across which a regiment could have advanced in line. And the mountains to the north, though still very lofty, were not jagged and rugged, but round and smothered in snow.

We descended from the pass by a steep zigzag path, and encamped that night at a place called Shorshma-aghil, where there were a dozen unoccupied stone huts used by the shepherds in the summer months. Here I halted my party, while on the next day I reconnoitred the way ahead. It was not the intention of Government that I should do more than examine the Shimshal Pass from the north. The examination of the rest of the way from the pass to Hunza itself was to be carried out from the Indian side—from Gilgit—and was in fact carried out by Lieutenant G. K. Cockerill (now Brigadier-General Cockerill, M.P.) a year or two later. My part was to examine from the northern side other passes farther west leading into Hunza, and only finally to come down through Hunza when all passes leading into the country had been examined.

I descended the valley for about eight miles, nearly to its junction with the valley of what is known in Hunza as the Shimshal or Shingshal River. As far as I went the path was fairly easy as the hill-slopes were gentle, but farther on the mountains became much more precipitous. The Hunza men kept saying that there were very difficult gorges ahead. And this was amply confirmed by Cockerill, from whose description I should gather that the gorges in that valley were about the worst in the whole Himalaya.

But as it happened, this difficulty, instead of interfering with my plans, exactly suited them. It gave me the excuse for turning back and going round by another way, and so examining another route into Hunza—anothe route which might be possible for Russian partie to enter the country by. So, as I looked at the t rific mountains ahead, and as I listened to the Hunza men expatiating on the difficulties which would be encountered, I said it was evident that this was no proper road for the envoy of the Queen of England to proceed by, and I must go back and find a more fitting road into the country. And just at this point I was met by the official sent to meet me, a fine tall man who spoke Persian and had fifteen men with him. He said he wished to be of every assistance to me.

And when I told him of my decision to go round by the Taghdumbash Pamir he agreed at once—much to my relief—and said I might do what I liked.

He brought with him a letter from the Hunza chief, Safder Ali Khan, in which the chief said he wished to afford me every assistance, so that Durand's visit had been more successful than he had thought. And Sultan Beg, the official, told Shahzad Mir on the way back with me to my camp that the Hunza people wished to be friendly with the British, and as the Kirghiz were also friends of the British, the Hunza men would not harm them any more but be friendly to them. From my camp I wrote a letter to Safder Ali, thanking him for his assistance, and saying that I was going round by Taghdumbash Pamir, and I sent with it a present of a fine robe, a turban, and a Kashmir shawl. I also gave the official a Kashmir sheet and twenty rupees; and a rupee each to his men. And he gave me 120 lbs. of flour and butter. Sheep and goats were also to have been given, but these had not arrived. After the exchange of civilities I told Sultan Beg he might take his leave, and I returned over the Shimshal Pass on the 17th.

The next day I passed through Darwaza again and caught up Turdi Kol and the Kirghiz. This time the commander of the outpost was full of politeness and came out some way to meet me. And I took on three Hunza men with me to show Turdi Kol how friendly the Hunza people now were. He was completely satisfied, and all the Kirghiz were delighted at the evidences they saw of the Hunza men's change of attitude. Turdi Kol's opinion of us had greatly risen. He told me that our arrangements were "straight and good." And great relief came upon him.

Thus ended satisfactorily my visit to the raiders' stronghold and exploration of the Shimshal Pass. It now only remained to investigate the passes leading from Taghdumbash Pamir into Hunza, and then return through that country to Kashmir and India.

CHAPTER XI

MEETING THE RUSSIANS

RETRACING my steps to the Yarkand River I found the very capable Jan Mohamed Khan with more supplies, and also letters from India waiting for me at Chong Jangal, so that complicated as the arrangements had to be they had all worked out satisfactorily. Among the letters was one from Government, informing me that Captain Grombtchevsky was approaching the Indian frontier by way of the Pamirs. And a few days later as I was marching down the broad open valley of the Yarkand River, a well-dressed, cultured-looking Andijani—that is, an inhabitant of Russian Turkestan—rode into my camp bearing a letter in Turki from Captain Grombtchevsky himself, saying he had heard I was in the neighbourhood and hoped I would visit him in his camp, which was only a day's march off and on the route I was following.

This was not exactly a surprise, for the letter from Government had forewarned me. But it was an exciting event, also delightful in prospect; for two Europeans always find it a joy to meet one another in the depths of Asia. We had opposite views on political matters. But that counted for very little and only made the meeting all the more piquant. Besides, there was the curiosity to know what he was like and what he was about, and how he set about what he was about.

I replied in Persian and English, saying I was glad of the opportunity of meeting so distinguished a traveller, and that I hoped to be with him the next day. On October 23 I marched towards his camp, keenly excited to see him and his arrangements. Ascending the narrow valley of the Ili-su on rounding a spur I saw just in front of me an encampment of three or four small tents, and as I rode up a tall, fine-looking bearded man in Russian uniform came out to meet me. This was Captain Grombtchevsky, who in the previous year had made the adventurous journey into Hunza itself. He was very frank and cordial in his welcome, and he introduced me to his companion, Conrad, a German naturalist. As a guard he had seven Cossacks, and besides these there were a few Kirghiz and Andijanis.

We had a short talk together, and he then asked me to dine with him after I had camped and unpacked. This dinner was a very substantial meal, and the Russian plied me generously with vodka. At the start he laughingly said that he was very annoyed with me, as before he had left St. Petersburg he had marked down those parts of the frontier region which had not been explored by Europeans, and now, just as he was entering an unknown region, he comes across an Englishman who has explored the whole ground. I could only reply how much I admired his audacity in venturing into Hunza last year. He said, Yes, he had had an adventurous time and had only got out by giving the chief everything he had, including his Cossacks' rifles. And he warned me not to give the chief a single thing he asked for, as if I gave one thing on his asking for it he would go on asking for more and more till he had got everything out of me. This warning I afterwards bore in mind to good purpose.

As the dinner progressed Captain Grombtchevsky talked more and more freely. He said that the English were the rivals of the Russians, but, he added, turning to Herr Conrad, "I hate the Germans a hundred times more than I hate the English." He became very frank, too, about the invasion of India. He said we English might not believe the Russians really intended to invade India, but he could assure me that the Russian Army—officers and men—thought of nothing else. He then called his Cossacks to the door of the tent and asked them whether they would like to invade India. And, of course, they gave a cheer and said they would like nothing better. I said that that was all very well, but how were they going to do it? Let us look at our respective positions in Asia. In India we were surrounded by mountains. In Central Asia the Russians were in an open plain. We had several railways right up to the frontier and a railway down it. The Russians had only a single railway. Our vulnerable points were strongly fortified. They had no fortifications. They talked of getting hold of the Amir of Afghanistan and the frontier tribes, and turning them on to the plains of India with promises of loot; but what about our turning them on Central

Asia with promises of the loot of Bokhara, Samarkand, and Tashkent?

All this was bluff, but it quite answered its purpose of showing we had our end up. And when I put my final question as to how the Russians were going to transport and supply their army when away from any railway they would have to cross deserts and mountains, the Russian could only reply that the Russian Army went wherever it was ordered to go and did not trouble about supplies and transport. And a good laugh closed the controversy.

The following day I returned his hospitality. Brandy was the only potent liquid I had with me, so I half filled a glass with it and was going to add some water, but he was shocked at the idea and stopped me at once. He did not realise that brandy is not the same thing as the comparatively mild vodka. He told me a lot about life in St. Petersburg, and what a good time he had had there. He belonged apparently to the Turkestan Administration, and was what we would call a military officer in civil employ. But, unlike most of his fellow-officers, he had a love of adventure and so got himself employed on these expeditions. He explained to me that it was very unusual with Russians to care for exploring, and anyone who did care for it was made a great deal of. For instance, the Tsar himself had sent for him before each of his expeditions and made him explain all his plans. Unless some such encouragement were given, no Russian would think of exploring. I told him that with us it was exactly the other way round.

Every obstruction was put in the way of exploration, or the whole army would be careering over Central Asia. Not even the Viceroy had asked to see me before either of my journeys.

He asked me many questions about our Indian troops, and hoped I would let him see my Gurkhas parade. I was delighted at the chance of showing them off. So I had up the havildar and told him that in an hour's time he must turn out for inspection by the Russian officer, and go through the manual and firing exercises. I said that the reputation of the whole Indian Army was in his hands, as these were the first Indian troops the Russian had seen. He said, "Very good, Sahib, we will show the Russian what the Indian Army is like." And presently they turned out, very smart and clean. They were in the finest condition after all the hard work they had had, and had a splendid soldier-like look about them. And they went through their exercises with the finest precision. The Russian was delighted and quite taken aback. He said he had not realised that these were regular soldiers. He had imagined that Indian soldiers were irregular. And he asked me to congratulate them.

When I went to tell the havildar he said, "I know what the Russian officer has been saying: he has been saying how small we are; but you tell him we are the smallest men in the whole regiment and all the rest are taller than he is!"

I got the Gurkhas to go over and "fraternise" with the Cossacks; which they did, but came back disappointed. They said the Cossacks were neither equipped nor fed anything like so well as they were, and when they had offered to have a rifle match with them, proposing that Captain Grombtchevsky and I should each put up ten pounds, the Cossacks had refused—much to my own relief, for I was not so sure that my Gurkhas were very first-rate shots. The Cossacks were certainly nothing like as well provided for as my men were. But they were a very hardy-looking lot, and a good, cheery lot too. Grombtchevsky said he would parade them for my inspection, but I must understand that they were irregulars and not regulars like my men were.

Altogether I greatly enjoyed these two days with the Russians. Before we parted I wanted to give him something. But the only thing I had that I could spare was Monier Williams' book on Buddhism! I had been so deeply interested in it myself, I assumed he must, of course, be interested in it too. He said he could not read a word of it. But I told him that did not matter. He must get somebody to translate it to him when he got back to Russia. Probably that poor book about which I was so keen was the next day reposing at the bottom of the Yarkand River.

He, on his part, was much more generous to me. He presented me with an enormous Pamir sheep. It was one of a flock which he was taking with him to eat, but it had become such a pet he could not bring himself to eat it, so he gave it to me. I took him back with me to India and found a good home for him with some kind friends at a hill-station, and he lived for several years, affording a big crop of wool every year.

On the morning that I left the Russian camp I made my men form up and "present arms" to Grombtchevsky, and he made his men "carry swords" to me. And then we parted with warmest expressions of friendship. I met him next year, at the conclusion of his explorations, at Yarkand, and occasionally heard of him afterwards in various posts in Central Asia and Manchuria. But I have lost sight of him for many years now. Our meeting was an interesting episode, for it was the first occasion on which Russians and English had met on the actual frontiers of India.

* * * * *

On the following day I crossed the Kurbu Pass and gradually descended to the Taghdumbash Pamir. I was now in very different country from what I had lately been traversing. I was on what is called the Roof of the World. It was a succession of wide open valleys at a height of from 13,000 to 15,000 feet above sea-level and bounded by mountains 5,000 or 6,000 feet above them. There was no need here to be constantly seeking for a track: the ponies or camels could find a way anywhere. There was also plenty of grass, and brushwood for fuel, to be had. The chief drawback of the Pamir was the wind. It blew with terrible force all day. And at night the thermometer would fall below zero.

These Pamirs are chiefly remarkable as being the home of the great sheep the *Ovis Poli*. This is, indeed, the only region where the true *Ovis Poli* is found. They have horns of enormous size, one of a head presented to Lord Roberts measuring

78 inches. I have none of the instinct of the sportsman, and was always keener upon devoting the whole of my time and energy to exploration, but I digressed for once in a way from my main purpose and went after the *Oves Poli*, and had the joy of seeing them from a distance of only about two hundred yards. The size of their horns was amazing. It seemed incredible that an animal could have horns so huge. And they had an almost top-heavy appearance. But in spite of the weight the animals were quick and swift in their movements and much too alert for me.

The Kirghiz who inhabit this region were a rougher, more grasping lot than those I had met at Shahidula. Being just outside Hunza, and living in tents in wide open valleys, they were peculiarly liable to attack, and, indeed, were only able to remain there by paying blackmail to the Hunza chief. They were nominally under the dominion, or suzerainty, or tutelage, of the Chinese; but the Chinese were able to do nothing to protect them, and payment of the demands from Hunza was a necessity. The alternative was the loss of their flocks, or perhaps even of their own lives.

The exploration of the Khunjerab Pass, leading from the Taghdumbash Pamir into Hunza, presented no difficulty. The ascent to it was so easy that I could have ridden the whole way. But again, as in the case of the Shimshal Pass, and all other passes leading into Hunza, the difficulty lay on the other side. It was easy enough to reach the summit of any one of them from the northern side. But on the southern side were fearful gorges;

and these formed the real obstacle. I did not proceed down the gorges from the Khunjerab, for I had still another pass to explore, namely, the Mintaka, and it would be from there that I would finally enter Hunza.

I hurried on to this pass, for winter was coming on apace. It was now November 1, and in my camp that night the thermometer fell to five degrees below zero—a range of 120 degrees from a shade temperature of 115 degrees at Rawal Pindi, when I had started on my exploration. In those days I still kept up the custom of a cold bath, and there was a coating of ice on the bath almost immediately the water was poured out. By November 7 I was at the foot of the Mintaka, and as this was to be my last day with the Kirghiz I had to pay them up for transport and supplies furnished me and for various services rendered. I paid them liberally, and in addition gave the three leading men presents. But one of these, named Juma Bai, had the effrontery to return my present, saying it was not good enough. He was a truculent fellow, but I had to bring him to his bearings, so I sent the interpreter back with the cloth and tea—my present which he had returned—and told him to throw them into the river before Juma Bai's eyes, turn loose a sheep which Juma Bai had given me, and tell him that I was profoundly displeased! This had a marvellous effect, for all the rest of the Kirghiz proceeded to turn upon the wretched Juma Bai and soundly beat him for having insulted a guest. The other two headmen also came over to my tent to apologise and to express the hope that I was not displeased with them also. I said that, on the contrary, I was most grateful to them for the help they had given, and we parted on excellent terms.

Next day, November 8, we crossed our final pass, the Mintaka, 14,400 feet above sea-level, and at last entered Hunza itself. The exploration of the passes had been completed, and the rest of my journey was merely the return home. Hunza had already been visited by Colonel Lockhart's Mission four years previously, and by Colonel Durand in the present year. There was, therefore, nothing actually new to explore: I should be going over already trodden ground. Nevertheless, it was in many ways the most interesting part of my journey. For the gorges of Hunza are hardly to be surpassed, except, perhaps, by those in the Mount Everest region; and the people were some of the wildest and hardiest in the whole Himalaya.

CHAPTER XII

HUNZA

SOON after crossing the Mintaka Pass, which on the northern side was as easy as the rest, we came upon the gorges so characteristic of Hunza. The mountains seemed to rise perfectly sheer from the bed of the river. Obviously they were not absolutely perpendicular. But they rose for thousands of feet so precipitously that we had to bend our heads far back to look at their summits. All was on a stupendous scale and of granite solidity. And we ourselves were groping like ants in a land made for giants.

But the cold and the snow and ice and whiteness were now passed. And, stern and severe as the mountains were, the extreme austerity was left behind. The air became wonderfully warmer as we descended, and also, as we fell to lower altitudes, there was more in the air and life became easier. For months past I had been living at altitudes of at least 12,000 feet, and much of the time at 14,000, 15,000, and 16,000 feet; and occasionally I had been to 17,000 and 18,000 feet. Now we were descending to 10,000 feet, and every day going lower still. That feeling of languor and exhaustion and of not being fully up to the mark which we always have at high altitudes gradually passed off, and fresh vigour came into us as we descended lower and lower.

But what reception should we meet with from these men of Hunza? This was the anxious question that continually occurred to me. They evidently did not intend to be actually hostile, for at the first camping-ground I was met by a small official with twenty men to carry my baggage. But I was not sure whether they would be surly or decently friendly.

And I was in rather a delicate position, for I could not proceed without their active help. Baggage animals could not possibly be taken through those fearful gorges. I must be entirely dependent on men for the carriage of my camp stores and equipment. And the only men to be had were, of course, these men who were employed on the raids. There was a great uproar when the governor of the upper part of Hunza made the demand upon them to carry my baggage; and I could well understand their objections, for to carry fifty or sixty pounds of baggage for a dozen miles, up and down the numerous ascents and descents, and over the rickety wooden galleries made along the face of the precipices, can have had little attraction. But that was the only thing to be done, and I was but too thankful that I had not a larger party with me.

Then I had to be on my guard against the rapacity of the people and bear Grombtchevsky's warning in mind. As they lived by raiding, their ideas on the interchange of goods was different from ours. The morning after my arrival in Hunza territory the governor asked me for payment of the present of sheep and eggs he had given me on the previous evening, and he explained that he could not afford to give presents for nothing. I had to be firm from the start and refuse to give any such payment, though I fully intended to, and did, give him a present when we parted.

The following day we reached a place with a fort called Gircha, and here I was met by two men of very special interest. The first was Mohamed Nazim Khan, the half-brother of Safder Ali Khan, the chief of Hunza. And the second was Wazir Dadoo, the minister of the chief. Mohamed Nazim Khan was then a friendly, agreeable, but very timid young man who went about in fear of his life, for his father, mother, and two of his brothers had met with violent deaths at the hands of Safder Ali Khan. Wazir Dadoo was of a very different type. He was remarkably capable, with a strong, authoritative manner, and also great suppleness and diplomatic skill. He had all the geniality, readiness, and courtesy of a thorough man of the world, and it was a pleasure to talk with him. He appeared dressed in gorgeous robes which had been presented by Colonel Lockhart in 1886 to Gazan Khan, the then chief, who had subsequently been got rid of by Safder Ali Khan. And he informed me that Safder Ali Khan had sent his own half-brother to welcome me and make all arrangements for my comfort.

Mohamed Nazim Khan in 1892 succeeded his brother, and has ruled the country ever since, and shown consistent loyalty to the British Government. Thirty-three years after our first meeting and thirty years after he had become ruler of Hunza, I received here in a distant Kentish town, a little present and most friendly message from him. But when I saw him at Gircha he lived far too precarious an existence to be a cheerful companion, and Wazir Dadoo was the distinctly more impressive of the two. And comparing him with many of the highly educated ministers I afterwards met in the Native States of India—or Indian States, as they are now called—I am not at all sure that Wazir Dadoo was not more capable than them all. There was between him and them all the difference that there is between a wild animal and a tame animal. The wild animal has every hour of its life to depend on its alertness and aliveness: it is in consequence quick and vivacious, and instantly ready to cope with every varying situation as it arises. The tame animal is slow and dull in comparison. Wazir Dadoo had for me the interest of the wild animal. He had all his wits about him. He had the assurance of achieved success. He was in a position of great influence and authority. But he could only retain it by unflagging vigilance. A British Prime Minister leads a fairly precarious existence. He may be in power one day and swept out of it the next. If to these elements of uncertainty there were added the prospect of being pushed off a precipice as well as the loss of power, a British minister would then understand what was Wazir Dadoo's position. A small man would crumple up under such conditions. But Dadoo was not a small man. He was a really big man, and he rejoiced in the risk and the power. It was a pleasure to have to do with a man of this kind. All difficulties about the transport of baggage or about anything else vanished immediately. A very few words from him and everything was immediately arranged.

What surprised me most about him was his cheery geniality. Most other Asiatics I had met —except the Gurkhas—had been grave and sedate. But he was always ready with a laugh. He had plenty of dignity, but it sat easily and naturally on him and was not stiff and stilted. And most of the time he was with me he was talking and laughing like one whom we would describe as "good company." He was fond of sport, too, and of polo, which is a national game in Hunza. And though the word "raid" was taboo, I could quite imagine him thoroughly enjoying a raid. His successor, Humayun, a graver, but equally capable man, certainly did; and when some years afterwards I asked him to show me with a hundred men how he carried out a raid—for he had led raids himself—his eyes glistened, and he entered into the proceedings with such zest it was easy to see that the wretched Kirghiz and Turkestanis would not stand much of a chance against such a man at the head of such hardy, ready, alert men as these Hunza people were. Later again Humayun spoke to me with a sigh of the "good old days" of the raids. And I had the same feeling for him that I have for hawks. They at any rate have to keep themselves at the highest pitch of perfection, with every faculty keen and alert or they will starve. Hawks, indeed, do not kill their own kind, and raiders did. But the Hunza raiders had no desire actually to kill men. A dead man was of no use to them. It was live men they wanted for the ransom that could be got for them.

From Gircha we marched in a couple of days to Gulmit, where I was to be received by the chief—Safder Ali Khan. I only wish that my mind had not been so absorbed with the prospect of meeting him, for in those two marches I passed through scenery of the grandest description. All the way we followed the course of the Hunza River, which here cuts clean through the line of the great peaks. Here and there the valley would open out somewhat, and there would be patches of rough cultivation and a few dirty villages of stone-built houses. But often the road was only the roughest pathway leading along the side of stupendous cliffs, and the great peaks were unbelievably high above us. It was the very kind of mountain scenery I had been keenest to see when I first started into the Himalaya, but now I could pay little attention to it, for I was thinking almost entirely of my coming interview with the renowned chief of Hunza. And hearing that he was to receive me immediately on my arrival, I put on my scarlet full-dress King's Dragoon Guards uniform, and also made the Gurkha escort wear their full-dress green rifle uniform.

As we approached Gulmit a deputation met me to warn me that I must not be frightened if I heard firing: it was only a salute fired in my honour. When we arrived closer the guns began to boom—thirteen of them, which, I was told, they had heard was a general's salute. It was most gratifying to me, as I had never had a gun fired in my honour before. And when the salute had finished a deafening beating of drums began—dozens of them all being beaten with might and main by frenzied drummers. On the hillside hundreds of people were collected, and as I neared the chief's tent—for he was receiving me in a tent, as he was away from his capital, which is Baltit—I found a double row of wild, hard-looking men, armed with matchlocks and swords. Here I dismounted from my pony and advanced between the rows towards the chief, who was standing outside the tent.

I was surprised to find Safder Ali almost European in feature. He had quite a fresh complexion and reddish hair and an almost burly appearance. He wore a magnificent Indian brocade robe and a handsome turban, both presented to him by Colonel Lockhart, and he had both a sword and a revolver fastened to his waistband, while one man with a drawn sword and another with a repeating rifle stood behind him. He greeted me quite politely and asked after my health and if I had had an agreeable journey, and then led me into the tent—one which had been presented to him by Colonel Durand. And here I had to exercise a little diplomacy. I noticed that at the end of the tent was only one chair, and it was evident that he intended to sit in that himself, and leave me to sit upon the ground with the headmen. But I had been prepared for such an eventuality: I had brought a camp chair with me on the march. So I kept up a string of complimentary questions about the health of the various relatives of the chief, while I sidled in between him and the chair. At the same time I sent off a man for my own chair. As soon as it arrived I had it placed alongside the chief's, and we then sat down together. On ceremonious occasions ceremony has to be carefully attended to.

Our conversation at this first meeting was of a purely ceremonial kind. I thanked him for the help he had given me and for the cordiality of my reception, and he made the usual acknowledgment. All the time the headmen, in two rows, one on either side of the tent, squatted on the ground, were listening intently to each word. But as the conversation had to be translated first from Hindustani into Persian, then from Persian into Hunza dialect and back again in the reverse order, we had plenty of time to take stock of each other. I felt that I was being eyed with the same directness as children eye each other and eye strangers, and I knew that I should be summed up with the same sure intuition. It would have been disconcerting if I had thought much about it, but in my scarlet uniform and as representing my Government I had a quite sufficiently good idea of myself—and perhaps they saw this, and perhaps it was not all a misfortune that they did. With the chief I was not nearly as well impressed as I had been with Wazir Dadoo. He had nothing like the Wazir's ability, nor did he impress me with the same sense of power. He was shifty and nervous, and there was nothing in him to grip on to. As for the headmen seated in front of us, though they had strong, hard faces they had not that fierce, fiery look one sees in the tribes on the North-West Frontier. With all their hardness they had a look of patience and long-suffering. The life of the people of Hunza was, indeed, in those days a very hard one. In the midst of those stupendous mountains there was little land available for cultivation. They had to live on short commons for a great part of the year. And raiding their neighbours was, in fact, almost a necessity of nature. After half an hour of outward compliments and inward stock-taking of one another, I asked the chief's permission to withdraw to my camp, and as I left the Gurkha escort, in accordance with the plans arranged, fired three volleys in the air as a kind of salute to the chief.

Next day I paid the chief a visit for business purposes and brought with me presents for him, for his half-brother Mohamed Nazim Khan, and for Wazir Dadoo. And these I had handed to them before commencing business. He began by asking me why I had come into his country from the north. No other European had come by that way. Why had I? I replied that I could not claim the honour of being the first European who had come into Hunza from the north, for only a few weeks ago I had met a Russian who had told me he had entered Hunza by this very way; and where a Russian could go I presumed an Englishman could go also. Safder Ali said it was true Grombtchevsky had come to Hunza, but he had gone back immediately. I then explained that I had been sent to Shahidula to enquire about the raids on the trade route and was now returning to India through his country.

When Safder Ali paid me a long return visit on the following day I entered more fully into this matter. I said that subjects of the Queen of England had been attacked and their goods stolen, and Her Majesty was very angry. I had been informed that it was men of Hunza who had made these raids, and if he wished to retain the friendship of the Queen I trusted he would take measures to restrain his subjects from committing them. I had assumed that he himself was ignorant of or disapproved the raids, but he immediately said straight out that they were made by his order: I could see his country, that it was nothing but stones and ice: if he could not raid his neighbours where could he get any revenue? I told him that anyhow he was not going to get his revenue from subjects of the Queen of England. He said that if Her Majesty wanted these raids stopped she must make up to him for the loss of revenue by paying him a subsidy. I said the Queen was not in the habit of paying blackmail, that I had left soldiers for the protection of the trade route, and he might try for himself how much revenue he would get now from a raid. Much to my astonishment, he burst into a roar of laughter. He said he could see through me like glass. Any other man with whom he had to deal, he said, would have promised him the subsidy, even if he did not intend to fulfil his promise; but I had told him straight that I would not.

This visit of the chief was followed by several

others. Wishing to impress him with our soldiers I made the Gurkhas do some drill before him. They were formed in line outside the tent, facing the chief and me sitting inside. They went through all their exercises very smartly, but when it came to the firing exercises and they presented arms and "fired" (of course, without any cartridges, either ball or blank) straight at us, Safder Ali was in terror. He had murdered his father and thrown two brothers over a precipice, and was evidently fearful of something happening to himself. He asked that the exercises might at once cease; and he would only permit the firing at a mark, which I had suggested, to take place when one cordon of men had been placed round him and another round the Gurkhas. Under these precautions he allowed the Gurkhas to fire volleys at rocks across the valley. The distance was about 700 yards. And when the people saw the bullet splashes all pretty close together, and appearing simultaneously, they were mightily impressed. Volley firing, I found, is always much more impressive to these people than firing by a single man, however accurate. But Safder Ali found firing at mere rocks rather dull, so seeing a man coming along the path on the opposite bank he wanted me to tell the Gurkhas to fire at him. I laughed, and said that would never do, as the Gurkhas were so accurate they would certainly hit him. "What does it matter if they do?" said Safder Ali; "he belongs to me." Though so nervous about his own life he was utterly callous of other people's.

On these visits to me in my tent Safder Ali kept

asking me unblushingly for one thing after another —even asking me for the tent itself and for my mule trunks. He asked also for some soap for his wives. Among the articles which I had given Wazir Dadoo had been some soap wrapped in silver paper, and Safder Ali's wives wanted some like this. But I had given away all I possessed. I had, in fact, exhausted all my presents, as I was now at the end of my journey. All I had left was the bare necessities of travel. And on principle I refused Safder Ali. I had given him a very handsome present, and I knew that if I gave in to his importunity I should be fleeced bare. He became very petulant and rude at my refusals. And eventually I had to tell him that I could not receive him any more, as he did not know how to behave himself towards the envoy of the Queen of England.

Wazir Dadoo, on the other hand, always behaved with dignity and decorum, besides being most agreeable to talk with. We discussed together the question of the raids, and he explained in a very reasonable and intelligible manner how it was they came about. He showed how there was really very little cultivable land or pasturage in Hunza, and that the people had not sufficient to eat, and the obvious remedy was to raid those who were more fortunately situated. The only flaw in the argument was that the chief took most of the proceeds of a raid for himself. Otherwise, these raids were merely a repetition of what has happened between the inhabitants of highlands and the inhabitants of lowlands all the world over.

By November 23, Balti coolies from Gilgit to carry my baggage having arrived, I was ready to start. Safder Ali had been so rude I had settled not to make a farewell visit to him. But just as I was starting he came down on foot to my tent and apologised for his behaviour. He said that he had not intended to be rude, and hoped that I would give a good report of him to the Viceroy. I replied that the Viceroy only wished to be on friendly terms with him, and if he also wished to be friendly that was all we wanted. He said that that was what he wanted—that and a subsidy! And so we parted. He was a poor creature, and in the last degree unworthy of ruling so fine a race as the people of Hunza.

The day after leaving Gulmit we reached Baltit, which is the capital of Hunza. Its principal feature was a fort palace built on the edge of a precipice, and behind this was a rugged mass of mountain rising in a succession of precipices 15,000 feet above it. And behind this was a row of rocky peaks almost as sharp as the spires of a cathedral. Down the valley, not twenty miles distant, was the magnificent mass of Rakapushi, over 25,000 feet in height. And away to the eastward were peaks of over 24,000 feet. In the whole world we could not find a more wonderful site for a mountain capital. And yet—as is, of course, quite natural—the people themselves were quite unaware that there was anything unusually remarkable about their valley. They thought, in fact, that the whole world was composed of giant mountains and tremendous precipices and rocky gorges. Away to the north was a big valley ruled over by the Tsar of Russia. On the east was another, of which the Chinese Emperor was the chief. To the south was Kashmir, and away behind it India, ruled by the Queen of England. And to the west were Chitral and Afghanistan. This to them was the whole world. Of it Hunza was the centre. And to Hunza all paid tribute—as the Hunza people called the blackmail they levied all round. It was a nice, comforting, self-satisfying theory to hold. And I am always reminded of these Hunza people when I read of us men on this tiny planet being the most important beings in the Universe.

Later on, many of these Hunza men were taken to India and their eyes were opened to some extent. But not altogether to their pleasure. The vast plains depressed them. They longed for their great mountains and to feel themselves snug and tight within them once more.

I was in a desperate hurry now to get on to Gilgit to see my own countrymen again, so rode from Baltit to Gilgit, sixty-five miles in two days, along mountain paths of the most execrable description, and passing round the butt end of Rakapushi, which rises in towering masses clear 19,000 feet above the valley bottom. My arrival at Gilgit was expected, but not quite so soon, and alarm was caused to the Kashmir Governor by the suddenness of my appearance at ten o'clock at night without any escort. But from Colonel Durand and Captain Manners-Smith I received the warmest welcome. And it was, indeed, a relief to find myself in comfort and security again.

with my task done and English friends to talk to. And talk I did. I could not keep myself in. And poor Manners-Smith, in whose room I was put, had to suffer me till five in the morning. All that had been pent up in me since I left Captain Ramsay at Leh nearly four months before—all my experiences with the Kirghiz, my adventures in the mountains, my talks with Grombtchevsky, my views about Safder Ali—had to be told and experiences compared. Only two years later, Manners-Smith was to gain the Victoria Cross in the gallant attack on Nilt, which opened the way to Hunza. But it is sad to think that this splendid man, who was then the very embodiment of physical vigour and pluck and dash, was destined to end his days in a nursing home in London from some unknown disease which slowly wasted away his strength.

Nowadays the journey from Gilgit to Kashmir is looked upon as a very commonplace affair. And it seems almost a waste of time to describe it. Dozens of Europeans perform it every year. And readers of E. F. Knight's "Where Three Empires Meet" are well acquainted with the country passed through. None the less, however often the journey may be undertaken, and however often the country may be described, it never ceases to thrill the traveller, and one never ceases wanting to describe it. And in those days, before ever Mr. Knight was there, before a regular road was made, when even the Indus had to be crossed by a rope bridge, and when the only track led by crazy wooden galleries along the sheer face of the most dreadful precipices, the journey was an experience well worth having and well worth talking about.

It is here that the Indus, rising in far-away Tibet and passing for hundreds of miles along the back of the Himalaya, cuts through the mountains and forms terrific gorges. And the river is a wonder in itself. Compressed tight between the mountains, it flows swift and deep and strong. Before those mighty peaks were it was. When they have dwindled to mere hills it still will be. While the mountains stand over it in granitic immobility it courses forward with a power that nothing can resist for long. Centuries of millenniums pass, but without cease it flows. And so tremendous is its power it is almost terrifying to watch. Yet we are fascinated by it; and as I watched it swirling, eddying by in deep and silent power, I thought of the vast glacier regions that it drains on the one hand, and on the other of the flat, hot plains that it will render fertile; and in spirit I went with it hurrying between the mountains, passing through forbidden countries, and at length emerging on to the sunny plains of India. A glorious adventure it would have been. But what was so easy for the river was hazardous, perhaps impossible, for men. At any rate, this was not the occasion for me to make the venture. And I turned from the river to those fearful cliffs and gorges which hem it in, and I rejoiced in a strength another than the river's. Puny, indeed, did one seem in comparison. And yet one's soul inevitably rose in response. Not less, but more stable still, must man's spirit be.

And crowning splendour of all was the massiveness of Nanga Parbat as it rises, in only fourteen miles, 23,000 feet above the Indus bed. Not even Mount Everest, K_2, or Kinchinjunga, presents so grand a sight. For though they are of greater height, Nanga Parbat being only 26,600 feet, yet they can only be seen at close quarters from a much higher altitude above sea-level. Here, on the Indus, we are right under Nanga Parbat, and yet at only between 3,000 and 4,000 feet above the sea.

I have perhaps enjoyed this glorious mountain more from my garden in Gulmarg—seen from a distance of eighty miles—mysterious in ethereal haze and compelling one's deepest soul to heaven. Here one was almost too close. The mass and weight was almost too overpowering. But yet one thrilled to see so grand a sight and know that earth could be so great. The whole scale of being was immeasurably increased. And having seen this last and greatest sight of all I rode on contentedly to Kashmir.

And here what a change immediately occurred! Not only did the scale of life appear diminished, but the whole tone was completely altered. Not only had the mountains diminished from Himalayan magnitudes to the proportions of the Alps, but the tone of austerity to which I had been so long accustomed was changed to one of geniality and warmth, and stern effort was replaced by tranquillity and peace. We descended rapidly through the pine forests from the snow of our last pass, and by evening had reached the shores of the beautiful Wular Lake. Boats awaited us here, and in the glow of sunset we were borne swiftly and easily on our way. No more effort was needed. Our hardships and our dangers were all over. We had only to loll back and enjoy the scene, and feel the satisfaction of another task accomplished. Something worth while had been done. What would bring us joy through all our lives was now our own.

A few days later I parted with my Gurkhas. Tears were in their eyes as we said good-bye. Before they left their regiment—so they now informed me—they had been told by their head native officer that if anything happened to me not one of them was to return alive to bring disgrace upon the regiment. They had been prepared for any sacrifice, but I had looked after them so well, they had had no hardships at all, they said, and they wished to thank me. Rough, sturdy little men they were, but a fund of tender sentiment lay beneath their rough exterior—and, in high moments like our parting, a true gracefulness as well. A peculiar sense of kinship strikes deep into us from experiences like this. On the surface life of every day there may be much in which we differ. But somewhere fundamental is a common tie between us and something tender which makes us every one akin.

CHAPTER XIII

THE SECRET OF THE HIMALAYA

ONCE more the Himalaya is shrouded in mysterious haze. The mountains have receded in the distance. I have pierced them through and through. I have stood under their highest heights. I have faced their sternest precipices. I have traversed their greatest glaciers. I have visited their remotest peoples. For the mystery they wore I went among the mountains. When I returned to the plains of India did I come back disillusioned? Did I find the hard facts and realities below what I had imagined? Was my ardour chilled, and did I never care to go again among them? Or, through the mystery, had I discovered some secret that was worth the knowing, and worth the toil and danger I had gone through to perceive it?

Such a secret I believe I found. And of it Shukar Ali was the embodiment. He had the hardest struggle for life. Owing to the cold and lack of rain his homeland produced but little. To earn a livelihood he had to follow caravans to Central Asia. For a mere pittance he had to trudge on foot across the highest passes, often in the teeth of icy blizzards, and when the altitude reduced vitality to a flicker. What were the hard realities of life he knew full well. What were its ills he had experienced in plenty; and of the good things life can give there were few he ever saw. Yet he did not add up the ills on the one side and the good things on the other, then strike a balance, decide which outweighed the other, and be comforted or depressed according to the result. What he did was to face the ills with courage and force himself to rise above them. And constant triumph made him bear a smiling face.

And this is the manner of the Himalaya also. Kashmir is an example. Its history is one succession of petty tribal wars and religious persecutions. Floods inundate the valley. Cholera has claimed its victims in hundreds a day. Famine has caused the death of thousands. Fire has destroyed whole quarters of a town. Earthquakes shake the very mountains. Scarcely ever is Kashmir without a scourge of some kind. And yet it is not on these evils we dwell when we think of Kashmir. For men are facing them squarely and rising triumphant above them. They have put down the internecine strife and established order. They have regulated the floods; checked the cholera; provided against famine; fought the fire; and withstood the earthquakes. And not only men, but animals, birds and insects, plants, and the very atoms of which mountains are made strive and struggle to turn chaos into order and make good prevail over evil. The struggle of the animals and plants with the climate alone—the frost and the heat, the ice, snow, and rain—is terrific, and their suffering terrible. And in addition animal struggles with animal and plant with plant, and animals and plants with one another.

Yet in the heart of this desperate struggle some agency must be at work subduing the chaos to order, moulding the shapeless to form, and creating beauty from horror; for good purpose is everywhere evident. From the rotting trunk of the decadent tree pure flowers and ferns spring up in abundance. And, net result of it all, so fair is the face of Kashmir that from countries most distant men journey to see it.

As we look at the Himalaya from such distance that we can see things whole and in their just proportion, the pain and disorder, squalor and strife, vanish into insignificance. We know that they are there, and we know that they are real. But we know also that more important, and just as real, is the Power which out of evil is ever making good to come. That there is a Power at work in the whole making for higher and forcing good out of evil is the true secret of the Himalaya. And the sign of its triumph is stamped on her face.

So the Himalaya remains to us a joy of which we never tire. The ill is but the evanescent. What stays for always with us is the grandeur, purity, and light. And these have power to draw us everlastingly to Heaven.

TRAVEL AND ADVENTURES.

A Wayfarer's Caravan. By **A. Alexander.** With a Foreword by **Viscount Gladstone, G.C.B., G.C.M.G.** "In Mr. Alexander we have another George Borrow. He takes a caravan and wanders through England, mixes among gipsies and has many strange adventures . . . a most stimulating book."—*Sphere.*

A Wayfarer's Log. By **A. Alexander, F.R.G.S.** "It is a book that reminds one of George Borrow. There is fighting in it, there is plenty of open air, and a jolly enjoyment of life which makes Mr. Alexander a stimulating companion."—*Daily Mail.*

The South Pole. By **Captain Roald Amundsen.** An Account of the Norwegian Antarctic Expedition in the "Fram," 1911–1912. Translated from the Norwegian by **A. G. Chater.** 2 Vols. With Illustrations and Maps.

The Naturalist on the River Amazons. By **H. W. Bates.** A Record of Adventures, Habits of Animals, Sketches of Brazilian and Indian Life, and Aspects of Nature under the Equator, during Eleven Years of Travel.

Out of the World North of Nigeria: Exploration of Aïr. By **Captain Angus Buchanan, M.C.** With an Introduction by **Lord Rothschild.** "A graphic account of long, weary months of travel and hardship in a desert country. . . . The author has an easy style and excellent descriptive powers which make his narrative delightful reading."—*Glasgow Herald.* With Illustrations and a Map.

Wild Life in Canada. By **Captain Angus Buchanan, M.C.** "There can be no question as to the popularity of this book. Naturalists, sportsmen, and all lovers of adventure will find the book profitable and entertaining."—*Pall Mall Gazette.* With Illustrations.

Three Years of War in East Africa. By **Captain Angus Buchanan, M.C.** With a Foreword by **Lord Cranworth.** "It forms a valuable contribution to the literature of the campaign, and incidentally provides a fine record of the work of the splendid corps to which he belonged."—*Army and Navy Gazette.* With Illustrations.

The Cruise of the "Cachalot" Round the World after Sperm Whales. By **Frank T. Bullen.** With 8 Illustrations and a Chart.

Journal of a Naturalist during a Voyage Round the World. By **Charles Darwin.** A record of observations made by a naturalist during a voyage round the world.

LONDON: JOHN MURRAY.